COLLECTING COLDITZ
AND ITS SECRETS

COLLECTING COLDITZ AND ITS SECRETS

A UNIQUE PICTORIAL RECORD
OF LIFE BEHIND THE WALLS

Michael Booker

Best wishes — The Christmas Attempt.

GRUB STREET • LONDON

Published by
Grub Street
4 Rainham Close
London
SW11 6SS

British Library Cataloguing in Publication Data

Booker, Michael
Collecting Colditz and its secrets : a unique pictorial
record of life behind the walls
1.Schloss Colditz (Colditz, Germany) 2.Schloss Colditz
(Colditz, Germany) – Pictorial works 3.World War, 1939-1945 -
Prisoners of war, German 4.World War, 1939-1945 –
Personal narratives, British 5.World War, 1939-1945 –
Personal narratives, German
I.Title
940.5'47243

ISBN 1 904943 08 X

Jacket and book design by Hugh Adams, AB3

Title page illustration: 'The Christmas Attempt', the most popular
Christmas card printed at Colditz in November 1942 and used by the
British prisoners.

To my wife Janet,
who has been there
from beginning to end

CONTENTS

FOREWORD

 Some forty years ago Michael Booker began a study on the history of the prisoner-of-war camp at Colditz. He then started a collection of Colditziana to illustrate his study, later to be used in many exhibitions, and has now made the entire archive the occasion for a gripping book. It disposes of two myths: one, that Colditz was a kind of bad hotel populated by larking schoolboys, the other that it was a hell-camp. Though in numbers the British predominated, he emphasises the comradeship of its multiraciality with French, Poles, and Czechs, and the shared patience and almost incredible ingenuity of all the escapes. As for details of the ways the Germans frustrated some of them, he quotes at welcome length from the diaries of their security officer himself. For years I had thought the Americans, who liberated us, simply sailed in. Booker shows what a hard time they had of it and what casualties they suffered. He shows also that (except when the SS either tried to, or did take over), the Wehrmacht Commandants observed the Geneva Convention. The book, with its wonderful illustrative material, would make an excellent war-game for the young in schools, indeed universities, with singularly little violence; a pitting against one another of wits, improvisation, endurance instead of bombs and guns; nothing over-romanticised; or demonised, except, on the German side, a lurking core of frightened sadists seeking to dominate the world and, if not, save their own skins; on the other side, some true heroes determined to get out in order to help destroy them; and many of the rest on both sides keeping a low profile and hoping, even planning for a better world. I feel as honoured to praise this book as I did when privileged to assist in taking the BBC news off the radio hidden in the attics, alongside the amazing glider, which was never called on to fly but, reconstructed after the war, proved that it would indeed have flown.

Michael Burn, 2005

ACKNOWLEDGEMENTS

There have been so many who have encouraged or helped to make the collection what it is today.

During the early stages of my research, I didn't realise how fortunate I was when I made contact with Reinhold Eggers, who was the security officer of Colditz. It was he who not only started the archive for me in earnest but also gave me the support to develop and expand it. My other main contact was Benji Stewart-Walker, a prolific escaper who ended up in Colditz, introduced to me by Dick Howe. Benji contributed a wealth of material.

This book has been on the back boiler for over twenty years. Two people have always encouraged me to put my work into print: first and foremost my wife Janet, who has helped and supported me from the beginning, in spite of the many intrusions into our life and home. Second my Australian friend Colin Burgess, who has always said there is room for just one more book in the Colditz library. Colin wrote the bestseller *Diggers of Colditz* with fellow Australian and Colditz veteran Jack Champ.

One high spot was when the collection was used in the BBC award-winning Colditz series between 1972 and 1974. I was invited to be part of the panel of consultants together with Colditz veterans Sir Rupert Barry, Jack Best, Dick Howe and Pat Reid. I remember them for their comradeship; sadly they are no longer with us. My thanks also to Brian Degas who devised the series and Gerald Glaister, the producer.

The TV series was followed by a highly successful Colditz exhibition at the Imperial War Museum in association with the *Radio Times*. My memorabilia formed part of that display. Over a quarter of a million paying visitors viewed the exhibition during 1974, and as a result of their donations the charity SSAFA received a handsome cheque. I would like to thank David Lay of the *Radio Times* and Christopher Dowling of the IWM and all their staff for making it the success it was. What exciting days they were.

David Ray and I go back many years. A teacher at a school where many a Colditz personality spent their informative years, David and I started a study group on Colditz in 1991 with great encouragement from the late Hugh Bruce.

Dick Howe, a charming man, was a mentor to me. He had been Big X, (the code name for the escaping officer), after Pat Reid made a 'home run'. Dick opened up so many doors for me. I still remember receiving a note he had written saying, "Would you come and pick up a box of junk from my office?" He had a big smile as he handed over to me the remains from the radio hide.

I was very fortunate to have known Sir Rupert Barry. He was truly one of life's gentlemen. Rupert gave me some unique items during the very early days.

Pat Reid of course stands out. We met on many occasions, particularly when he was writing *Colditz The Full Story*. I asked him once whilst we were travelling in a taxi if he would consider not putting Colditz into the title. Asking what I suggested instead I replied, "Grey Towers", reminding him that this was what the Polish prisoners christened the castle. Pat thought that it was a good idea, but the publishers naturally insisted on Colditz being in the title. Pat gave me a few gems and was active on the subject until the end.

I visited John Watton at his home in the Lake District. John was of course the talented Colditz artist, his work appearing in the book *Detour*. Compiled by the Canadian Jerry Wood, the illustrations were mainly by John. Initially he was not aware why Jerry asked him to produce so many drawings and in a letter to me in 1975 he wrote that Jerry had to join his band of 'Watton's slaves', so named because of the odd jobs they did for payment or drawings. John generously gave me a number of drawings over a period of time and during my visit, knowing of my interest in Mike Sinclair, he gave me a pastel drawing of him, which now takes pride of place in my collection. He explained that he had copied this from his original in *Detour*. Unfortunately this had gone missing whilst with the publishers in 1946.

Douglas Bader had a reputation for using his tongue to good effect in war and post-war years. I found he was also a man with a sense of humour, and one who kept his word.

So far the men I have thanked have been officers. Of the other ranks two should not be forgotten. Both were different as chalk and cheese. Sidney 'Solly' Goldman and John Wilkins were each outstanding in their own way. Both have been guests at my home and I am proud to have called them friends. Solly, as he liked to be known, was in regular contact from across the Atlantic. He asked me to arrange a meeting with the Colditz Association as he had been given six months to live and was determined to make one last trip. They gave him an emotional reception, proof of the high esteem in which they held him. John I knew as a trumpeter at my local pub. This was long before I found out over a glass of beer of his extraordinary experiences at the castle. I am pleased to say I put their stories on record and remember them fondly.

Memories come flooding back of other veterans who have helped over the years, so many no longer with us. Amongst those in particular are Peter Allan, Dominic Bruce, David Cleeve, Gris Davies-Scourfield, Harry Elliott, Tommy Elliott, Francis Flinn, Howard Gee, John Hoggard, Mike Moran, Tony Rolt, Peter Winton and Jimmy Yule. Also the four Senior British Officers with whom I was fortunate to have made contact: Guy German, 'Daddy' Stayner, William Broomhall and Willy Tod. My thanks also to Hamish Blair-Cunningham, (the hilarious incidents of the 'corked' wine and chicken bones are always remembered), Martin Francis (the Colditz glider man, who knows more than anyone about this subject), Graham Reynolds, a collector extraordinaire, and Colonel Sinclair and Professor Storie-Pugh, both of whom filled in vital parts of the jigsaw puzzle.

I have also been helped by veterans from all over the world. The Polish contingent is represented by the ex-escaper Onyszkiewicz, a wonderful man whom I met in the early days in unusual circumstances. It was he who introduced me to Antoniowicz, a Colditz officer and escaper, and the Sikorski Museum. From there I met Giertych, the first Polish escapee, and corresponded with Colonel Dunin-Borkowski, the tunneller. All great Polish patriots.

My French contacts were René Bardet, who corresponded to me on his brave and daring double life in Colditz; Jean Brejoux, the father of the French tunnel; Duquet, and of course Fredo Guigues, Big X

of the French. An extraordinary character.

Of the Dutch I must thank van Doornick, Larive and Steinmetz. I still have fond memories of a trip to the castle when Jack Hageman and his son Philip were with us.

Also the Czech Ivo Tonder, who made England his home. This very brave man, whom I had the privilege to meet, was so unassuming and would do anything to help people. He is sadly missed.

The Americans and in particular the 'Fighting' 69th Infantry Division have a special place in the Colditz story and its liberation. My very good friend, the late Alan Murphey, was my eyes and ears on the American involvement. Alan was with Robert Miller, Walter Burrows and Francis Giegnas, all them PFCs when they walked into Colditz on 16 April 1945 and liberated the prisoners. For this they received the Bronze Star. I have only traced Murphey and Miller. It would be gratifying to trace the other two or their relatives.

Mention should also be made of PFC Robert Muckel, whom I have traced as the GI who walked in and out of the castle before the famous four. Robert kindly gave me his story.

I would also like to thank all the other Americans for their help, in particular Clarence Marshall, late of the Fighting 69th veterans committee. Also the men of 9th Armored Division and 273rd Infantry who liberated Colditz, in particular veterans Armstrong, Hoffman, Kent, Kidd, Kutzmonich, Meadows, Oliver, Sarube, Sturm, and Telenko, Verdugo and Wegener, all of whom have provided either reminiscences or mementos.

The US Army Record Office I acknowledge for the photographs relating to the liberation of Colditz. Our own Imperial War Museum as usual has been very helpful.

It is right that mention be made of Col and Frau Prawitt who supplied me with a number of documents. Also Peter Hofmann, a Colditz guard, and possibly one of the last links to the German story.

I would also like to thank Michael Burn, for his excellent foreword.

Last but not least, my thanks to Renata Lippmann at the Colditz Museum and Louise Stanley at Grub Street for her excellent work.

My sincere apologies to those I may have missed out from over the years.

INTRODUCTION

The year 2005 heralds the sixtieth anniversary of the liberation of the prisoner-of-war camp at Colditz Castle. It is also the fortieth anniversary of the start of my Colditz collection. To celebrate the liberation, which took place on 16 April 1945, I thought it appropriate to put my collection, and the mass of information I have collated over the years, into print. Prior to this it has only appeared at exhibitions and displays, or in magazines and books as individual items.

Accumulating this archive has been a rewarding and sometimes challenging task, and I have been lucky to have met so many veterans of that time. I now have hundreds of items relating to Colditz including artefacts, letters and photographs, all of which come together to give an amazing picture of what it was like to be in that environment.

Colditz Castle, which is in eastern Germany between Leipzig and Dresden, was a unique place; an imposing fortress containing so many important Allied personnel during World War Two, which has become one of the most well-known prisoner-of-war camps of all time.

The first proper castle on the site was built in 1083 and given to Wiprecht von Groitzsch; the town of Colditz being established after 1200. This castle was destroyed by fire in 1430, and rebuilt in 1464 by Ernst of Saxony. Again, in 1504, a fire claimed the castle and much of the town, and in 1506 reconstruction started again. In this period it was converted into a hunting lodge. During the early seventeenth century Duke George of Saxony gave his wife Sophia a neighbouring wood around which he had a wall built and named it the 'Tiergarten'. This became well known to the POWs, or at least the ones who managed to escape, as they would invariably pass through it on their escape route. It is now a beauty spot, where many members of the public take walks.

Legend has it that the Countess Rocklitz, who lived locally, enjoyed a 'liaison' with the Duke at Colditz and they met via an interlinking tunnel. This possibility was explored by the British prisoners with the help of Professor Storie-

Taken from a set of *notgeld* issued in Colditz in 1921. The 50pf notes illustrate the castle destroyed after an invasion in 1430 by the Hussites, and in 1637 by the Swedes.

A card from the 'Germany Awakes', series of 1933. The Swastika sun is shown rising over Schloss Colditz.

Card issued on 12 July 1938 commemorating the national competition of the SA in Berlin. This is postmarked Colditz 8 October 1938.

Pugh and MI9. Unfortunately no tunnel was ever found.

After this time the castle started to fall into disrepair and in 1800 it was turned into a poorhouse. From 1829 Colditz Castle was used by the state as a lunatic asylum. This lasted almost a hundred years before its closure. Contrary to some beliefs, the castle did not contain prisoners of war during World War One, as it was still an asylum.

The castle opened again in 1933 as the worst type of asylum, not for lunatics, but for opponents of the Nazi regime. Run by the SA, the private army of Rhöm, called the Brown Shirts because of their uniform, it was known as a 'wild camp', and was one of a number set up by the SA under Rhöm. The SS or Black Shirts under Himmler, responsible for the security of the country, gave tactical approval but kept a low profile at the 'Shooting House', the building of a local gun club, which was to come to prominence during the war.

For those held in the castle as a concentration camp in 1933 conditions were primitive and cruel until Berlin received complaints from a town normally fairly tolerant. There were also allegations of corruption. The prisoners were being hired out to local businesses to work for them. The execution of Rhöm (by order of Hitler) in 1934, saw the demise of the SA. When Goering, as head of police, handed control of all concentration camps to Himmler, some 'wild camps' were closed. Prisoners not released were sent to regulation concentration

Parade of the Arbeitsdienst. The Compulsory Labour Service parading for inspection and work within the inner court-yard of Colditz Castle. Their accommodation was later to be used by the POW population. The labour force was conscripted for a period of time to work on the road and other building projects. For this they received a uniform, food, accommodation and comradeship, with the thanks of the Nazi party. (*Colditz Museum*)

Celebrating the Nazi Party, 1933. Members of the Brown Shirts or SA, which include guards from the castle concentration camp, march through the town of Colditz. Note the SS officer represen-tative marching behind the mounted SA leaders and standard bearer.

camps. Colditz prisoners were moved to Sachsenburg whose prison population was reduced to accommodate them.

With the castle once again empty the frugal living conditions were ideal for the Arbeitsdienst or Compulsory Labour Service. All young men within the German Reich had to work for their country without pay. The cobbled streets of Colditz resounded to marching men, spades across shoulders, singing their patriotic songs as they walked to work or drove past in trucks.

On 31 October 1939 the castle was made ready to receive Polish prisoners of war. General Wolff of Four Military District hired it on an instruction from the Military High Command in Berlin. Built on a steep gradient, it dominated the town of Colditz which was located in Army Area Group C. Originally designated officer camp (Oflag) IVC, it was known to senior POW officers and the POWs, together with future generations, by the Germanic name Colditz. Polish Lieutenant Adamowicz was the first registered prisoner.

The German High Command or OKW had not been happy opening the castle as a POW camp at this stage, but the unexpected surge of Polish prisoners in 1939 caused acute overcrowding in camps and forced Colditz to be used as a transit camp. Nonetheless the German Security Services still made use of its facilities as a Sonderlager or 'special camp'. Until 1943 more than 1000 prisoners were at the camp, from 1943 onwards 2-300 (British).

There is evidence to show that some prisoners initially entered the castle without being registered for interrogation. The SS had a 'black book' in which were listed the names of those they wanted to take into custody. They also held those alleged of anti-German crimes being laid against them by 'volksdeutch' (ethnic Germans) in Poland. These were taken to the camps for interrogation and to look for evidence. If evidence was found, they would be sent to a concentration camp, if not, a prisoner-of-war camp.

In 1940 the first Polish ex-escapee prisoner arrived at the camp, and he was followed not long

Card posted by Lieutenant Adamowicz.

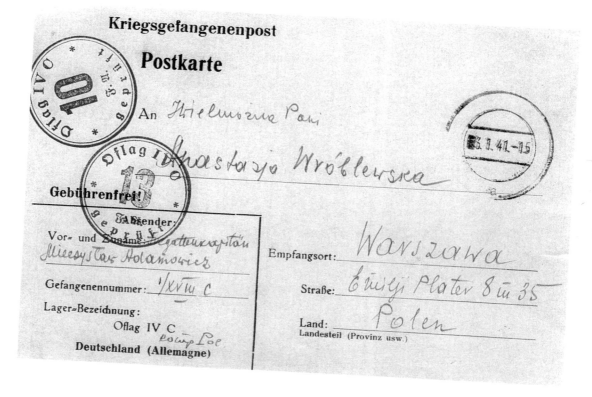

Postcard of Colditz Castle sent in 1943 by a British officer to his wife.

after by three Canadian RAF officers, then six British Army officers, including Pat Reid. Colditz was by now classified as a Straflager (punishment camp). In the camp it really just meant that life was stricter – there were more roll calls and a closer eye was kept on the prisoners.

One Colditz myth that seems to have survived from this time and should be mentioned is that there is no record of Goering ever having visited Colditz, which has been thought to have been the case many times over the years.

Post-war Colditz Castle was used as a hospital, for diseases of the ear, throat and eye, and to cure internal diseases suffered by Russian officers. There was also a nursing home for about 400 patients. This was closed in 1996 when an association was founded to establish the castle as a cultural centre.

OFLAG IVC
BRIEF TIMELINE OF STATUS DURING WW2

October 31 1939 TRANSIT CAMP	November 1940 STRAFLAGER (Punishment camp)	1943 SONDERLAGER (Special camp)	1945
Began to receive prisoners captured in the Polish campaign. Also used to relieve overcrowding in other camps.	Received the Spangenberg three (RAF officers) and Laufen six (Army) escapees. These were followed by other escapees and prisoners that were difficult to handle and classified 'anti-German'.	Began to receive prisoners under sentence of death (Czechs etc.), political prisoners and hostages for Hitler (Prominente).	Influx of French prisoners moved from camps after the Allied advance.

• ONE •
WELCOME TO COLDITZ

Oflag IVC at Colditz Castle was solely a transit camp until the end of 1940, when it took on the additional role of a 'Straflager' or 'punishment camp' with the arrival of the first escapees and anti-Germans. In time there were to be several hundred of them.

The Polish navy officer Jedrez Giertych, who appeared in the black book, was the first escapee to arrive at Colditz in 1940, having been previously held in two Sonderlagers for Polish officers at Silberberg in the Owl Mountains. Because of his escape activities at both camps he was put in one of the solitary confinement cells; a cold, stone cell with a wooden door. The furniture consisted of a bed and bucket. The cell was located under the covered walkway leading to the guard house, adjacent to the inner yard that housed the prisoners. His solitary confinement cell was to become the basis of the camp for escapees – known as Sonderlager Colditz.

Because of the morale boost it gave to the existing prisoners, his presence soon being discovered, Giertych was returned to the Owl Mountains. He was soon involved with others in another escape attempt. This was discovered under suspicious circumstances.

A prominent escaper at Silberberg was Lt Onyszkiewicz. One of his crimes that led him to being held there, and subsequently moved to Colditz, apart from his escaping activities, was the fact he would comment unfavourably to his fellow prisoners on the German press reports.

Onyszkiewicz wrote: "Having been sent to the Polish Sonderlager at Silberberg I was involved in 'activities'. After an escape attempt all the prisoners were sent to Colditz."

These included General Pisker, C-in-C of the Lublin Army, and Admiral Unrung, commander of the Peninsular of Hel. Unrung had been a respected World War One submarine commander in the German navy.

The first of the British Commonwealth prisoners to arrive at Colditz were three Canadian RAF officers: Keith Milne, Howard 'Hank' Wardle and Don Middleton. They had escaped from Spangenberg in August 1940, which was probably one of the first escapes of the war. Milne and Middleton had escaped as German workmen and Wardle by scaling an enclosure. They were all recaptured and sent to Colditz.

Colditz, March 1941. Front row, from left to right: Lt J. Ponewcjynshi (Polish), unknown Polish officer, Lt J. Giertych (Polish navy), Lt Peter Allan, unknown French officer, Major E. Baranowski (Polish officer who died in Italy after liberation), Capt R. Howe, unknown French officer. Back row, from left to right: Lt A. Onyszkiewicz (Polish), Lt L. Bialy (Polish).

he castle during the day. Enclosed by a major in a letter to ngland, it was returned having been refused by the censor.

Group photograph taken at Colditz in mid-December 1940 including the first three Canadians to arrive there. From left to right: Barton, Milne, H. Wardle, T. Elliott, Storie-Pugh, Middleton, G. Wardle.

Instructional card to inform relatives of new address, Oflag IVC Colditz. Issued to Sub Lt Geoffrey Wardle, known as 'Stooge', because of his regular activity in watching (stooging) the guards during escape attempts. Captured after the sinking of HMS Seal, he was involved at Colditz in the Gephard office escape, canteen tunnel escape and an escape from the Polish orderlies' quarters.

Christmas 1940 saw twenty-three British and Commonwealth officers in residence at Colditz. This included a Czech RAF pilot and the Senior British Officer Lt Col Guy German.

The prisoners came either by coach, truck, and car, or by train. The latter was the most common form of transport and the new arrivals usually disembarked late at night at the small railway station on the edge of town.

On arrival and dragging their belongings, they faced a walk along a cobbled road to the Adolf Hitler bridge that spanned the River Mulde. There they would get their first full view of the castle, dominating the town from a high gradient, cast in deep shadows by the spotlights illuminating the outer walls.

The cobbled yard where the prisoners took their exercise was starved of light because of the high surrounding walls. The dark rooms were damp and cold.

The name Colditz was well known in the other POW camps, but many thought it was the name of a concentration camp. This was mainly because they had not known anyone ever come back from there. Of course, this wasn't the case, but it was certainly not a place of comfort. However, despite being an 'escape-proof' fortress, there were to be over thirty successful escape attempts over time.

Of his arrival the legless fighter ace Douglas Bader wrote: "My immediate reaction to Colditz…was not perhaps as violent as you might think. I arrived in the late evening when the castle was floodlit and as one marched up from the station it looked just like a fairy castle."

On crossing the bridge the prisoners then bore left to walk up a sloping cobbled street named Baderstrasse to the castle road. They were then faced with a steeper climb to the castle entrance. Having already suffered hardships and hunger before arrival at the station, they faced a walk of about a mile to arrive at the castle exhausted, completely demoralised and not knowing what the future held.

Their arrival at Colditz was not pleasant. Separated from the Polish prisoners, they were told by sadistic guards that they were to be shot. The following morning at dawn they were taken from their room, escorted to the park area and told to stand against the dividing wall of the park. They waited, anticipating a bullet in the back, until they were escorted back to their room by highly amused guards.

It was therefore with great relief, after their harsh treatment, that they welcomed the arrival of their new comrades, the 'Laufen six', two days later. They were six Army officers, including Pat Reid, all of whom had been recaptured after the first tunnel escape by British Army officers in the war, and sent to Colditz as a punishment.

Peter Storie-Pugh   P.R. Reid   Dick Howe   Pete Allan   Kenneth Lockwood

Walter Morison, who with Lorne Welch escaped from Luft III dressed as Luftwaffe and attempted to steal an aircraft from a military airfield, wrote: "Coming from Sagan to Colditz was a culture shock. A few people had gone there but none had returned to tell the tale."

On arrival at Colditz the escort could only leave after it was verified that the OKW had authorised the prisoner's entry to the castle. This was an important factor as illustrated later. On being signed for by the camp or security officer, the prisoner was led into a room in the outer courtyard. Usually if not being used, the nearest

The floodlit castle at night.

room would be the officers' mess just to the left of the entrance.

The prisoner was there handed a form M/0162 on which was printed a list of forbidden items. The punishment would then be explained (solitary confinement) if any of the items listed were not handed in and found during the search. There would then follow a search of the prisoner and his luggage. Depending on the category of the prisoner this could either be a general or a strip search.

A perforated receipt form listed details of items taken and a copy was handed to the prisoner.

A search could include an internal examination if the prisoner was thought dangerous. The Germans were aware of the various methods of transporting escaping material, including a holder known as a 'cripper' that was pushed inside the rectum with a piece of cotton or string attached.

If the search found nothing, the prisoner was then escorted to the prisoners' yard. There he would either come under the wing of a friend or member of his regiment. Those unknown and arriving alone would be treated

The Laufen six. So called because of their tunnel escape from an Oflag at Laufen. This is recorded as the first tunnel escape by British Army officers in the war. From left to right: Capt Harry Elliott, Capt Sir Rupert Barry, Capt Pat Reid, Capt Dick Howe, Lt Peter Allan and Capt Kenneth Lockwood.

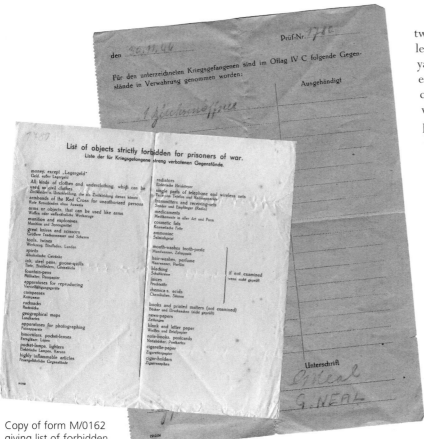

Copy of form M/0162 giving list of forbidden items, which was handed to prisoners on arrival. (*Neal*)

Perforated copy of receipt form M/0162 for items surrendered by Gerald Neal. A reference number 1780 was written at top right by the company stores officer Furtich and signed for at bottom right and a copy was handed to the prisoner. (*Neal*)

twisting stone staircases with edges worn away led to the prisoners' quarters. The prisoners' yard was cobbled with an incline from the entrance. It had the radius of a large tennis court and with tall buildings on four sides, it was only the midday sun that allowed the prisoners the luxury of sun-bathing. Fortunately many of the occupants were young and fit and the morale throughout the camp was high.

The age of the prisoners ranged from twenty and a half (by John Davies at his arrival in April 1941 but later taken over by Coran Purdon in June 1943), to a seventy-four-year-old Polish soldier.

By June of 1943 Colditz had become a Sonderlager for British Commonwealth, and Czech RAF and later the Free French and Americans. It is interesting to note that from an average population of 368 at Colditz during the Sonderlager period, 7% were RAF, 7% Navy, 81.5% Army, with the others (relatives of the Royal family etc) making up the balance.

There were four categories of prisoners, as designated by the Germans. The prisoners' acceptance into the camp by the Commandant was very strict. Only after the OKW had considered each individual or group, on the advice of the security services, were orders issued for their admission to Colditz.

The most important category was the **Prominente**. These were considered Hitler's hostages in order to give him bargaining power later in the war. They consisted of relatives of the British Royal family, close or distant relatives of important statesmen and military leaders, and also included General Bor-Komorowski, leader of the Polish Home Army who led the uprising against the Germans in Warsaw in 1944.

It has been suggested, even by German sources, that there was a second grade of Prominente including Bader, MacKenzie, Rothschild and other prominent prisoners including the VCs, such as Charles Upham. It has also been mooted that such people had restricted movement and regular checks. I have found no verification of this and certainly there has been

with suspicion and escorted until checked through interrogation by the British security officer and Senior British Officer. The new arrival would then be invited to join a mess for distribution of food, if he so desired.

The prison camp conditions were adequate for the British in respect of space, once the other nationalities had been moved to their permanent camps. Prisoners recall the thick damp cold stone walls, and small windows in deep recesses with bars that allowed little light to filter through. The electricity was shared with the town, which took priority but still complained of the amount used by the camp. There were often electricity cuts through overloading and when available it was low voltage, making reading very difficult.

Overcoats were the order of the day in winter and many stayed in bed for warmth, even though the heating was called adequate by the visiting Protecting Power Representatives. Steep no mention of restrictions by those concerned, except where they affected the rest of the camp as well. However, the Prominente as a whole were specially guarded and there were more roll calls for them than the other prisoners. Also the guards were told to keep a closer eye on specific people. Romilly, Churchill's nephew, was the only one whose movement was restricted though, the others were merely watched more keenly but still allowed freedom of movement.

Earl Haig, son of Field Marshal Haig wrote: "My impression of Colditz was that it was on the whole a very inspiring camp to be in because the spirit of all the officers there was terrific. We were short of food in the last winter and the Prominente were specially guarded and suffered certain restrictions which other officers did not have, which made things worse."

Next category was **Escapees**. There were, however, a number of persistent escapees who never got sent to Colditz, as the veterans will only be too quick to admit. Two that come to mind are of course Lt Cdr James Buckley of the Fleet Air Arm and Sqd Ldr Roger Bushell, who were both eventually killed during escapes; Buckley in '41 and Bushell in '44.

One of the most famous tunnel escapes was

the 'Eichstätt' that resulted in the recapture of sixty-five officers, who were sent en masse to Colditz in 1943. It was the largest escape so far of the war. Hitler was furious about the manpower involved and his anger was responsible for the terrible slaughter of prisoners after Operation Escape 200, the number of prisoners expected to escape from Sagan in 1944, known post-war as The Great Escape. Only two arrived at Colditz from that escape; both were Czech airmen, Ivo Tonder and Freddie Dvorak, like the other Czechs in Colditz, under sentence of death. It was thought by the security services that these two had important information on the Czech Home Army and subsequently on the 1942 Heydrich assassination, which Tonder said he encouraged.

The general attitude held by the young men of Colditz to escaping could best be illustrated by some of the letters I have received over the years on the subject.

Geoff Wardle: "I was captured when HMS *Starfish* was sunk. Sent to Spangenberg I was told by the Commandant that if I escaped I would be shot. If I escaped again I would be sent to a special camp! True to his word I ended up in Colditz."

John Hoggard: "I was sent to Sandbostal where I teamed up with three Royal Marine officers and started a tunnel. We recruited twelve more officers and used it in April 1942. I was out five days before being recaptured. Because of this and my general behaviour the Germans sent me to Colditz."

Peter Greenwell: "Having been in four camps I was sent to Colditz in July '43 for being outside without a guard."

Guy German, who was Senior British Officer at Colditz 1940/42: "My second visit to Colditz was in 1943 having been found leaving my last camp in a laundry bag." German had been such a nuisance to the Commandant that he had been sent back to his original camp, but after doing the same there, was sent again to Colditz.

It has been argued that other camps had equally as important escapes as the ones from Colditz. What needs to be noted is that many of these escapes –Eichstätt, Laufen and Sandbostal tunnels, the Warburg Wire Job, attempted theft

The eldest POW held at Colditz was seventy-four. Shown between two Polish officers, he joined the army aged seventy-one. Asked why, he replied, "I just wanted to help defend my country."

of German aircraft and others, were all masterminded by men who were later sent to Colditz because of these escape activities. So, in effect, Colditz was a kind of finishing school for great escapers.

The third category was **Enemy of the Third Reich**. A camp Commandant could dispose of a troublemaker, as long as he could convince the OKW. A good example was Douglas Bader, moved from camp to camp because of his attitude towards his captors.

Lt Col German seemed to fall in both categories – escaper and troublemaker: "I was removed at Spangenberg as Senior British Officer as I refused to allow *The Camp* (a German propaganda newspaper) to be circulated. I said that whilst I remained in the camp I was the SBO. They sent me to Colditz where they made me the SBO."

Lt Col Stayner who took over as SBO from German in 1942 wrote: "I was giving active assistance to escapes in my camp, so I was sent to Colditz and took over from Guy German."

Lt Col Tod: "Having been in various camps the Germans thought I was difficult and sent me to Colditz as SBO."

Micky Burn, a Commando Captain awarded the MC at St Nazaire and remembered for his V sign on seeing a German film crew, which got through to Military Intelligence in England indicating the raid was a success, said: "Having been a friend of Unity Mitford in the thirties and meeting Hitler who gave me a signed copy of his book *Mein Kampf*, they thought I would be co-operative when captured. On refusal to go to a propaganda camp I thought I was being sent to Buchenwald. It was a pleasant surprise to arrive at Colditz."

The final group covers all other personnel who don't seem to fit in the above categories, and who seemed to have been sent to Colditz for no known reason. However, the Germans were very careful whom they sent to Colditz and always did have a reason, no matter how twisted it seemed. Two of the other ranks who appeared there, having been captured in the Middle East,

Other ranks (ORs) to arrive in Colditz, 1940. From left to right: John Doherty, Howard Gee (civilian captured returning from Czechoslovakia and suspected of spying by the Germans), John Smith, William MacKenzie, Sidney 'Solly' Goldman (famous OR, only one to be used regularly by escape committee), John Wilkins (senior OR, captured from HMS *Starfish* and held at Colditz for leading a mutiny against the Germans).

were Sidney Smith and Gerald Neal. On the capitulation of Italy they had been imprisoned, then Gerald got out for three days before recapture. Although sent to Stalag IVD he was then suddenly taken to Fort Königstein. On arrival he met Sid Smith who had been taken from Stalag VIIIB, and three other soldiers, all of whom had similar experiences, having been captured in the Middle East.

They were all looked after well but seemed to be alone in that great fortress. They were concerned that they might be shot, and it was with the arrival of a group of soldiers who were SAS or commandos and led by a Sgt Brown, that they thought their fate was sealed. The sergeant understood they were to be executed under the 'Bullet Order' issued by Hitler in October 1942 against 'terrorists'. This was a reference to commandos and other specialised units. Therefore, when the five soldiers were called to the Commandant, they were relieved to be told they were being sent to Colditz to act as orderlies.

There were two known incidents when escorted prisoners were actually refused entry to Colditz. Gerald Eppink from Holland wrote: "After the capitulation I was allowed home to my sawmill, it being essential work. In 1942 all soldiers were ordered back to the camps [no doubt to work camps]. Many of us hid with the Underground and I stayed on a farm. But one day I stayed overnight in my parents' house and was betrayed. This was May 1944. After time in a prison I was sent to Stalag IVB. Then a train under escort sent me with a small group of Dutch prisoners in similar circumstances to myself to Colditz. Arriving at the castle gate at 9pm both we and our escort were exhausted. Our entry was refused, apparently there was no written order received from the OKW. We were instructed to try a camp on the edge of town. This was the Shooting House where a Corporal Werppley was in charge. The camp there held about a hundred Dutch POWs and we were made welcome."

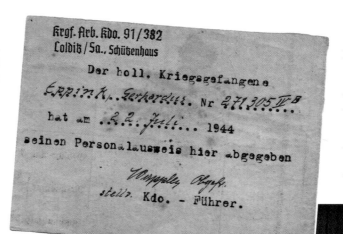

A pass issued to Eppink for 22 July 1944 signed by the camp Commandant Corporal Werppley. It shows the work commando number issued to the Shooting House, at that time known as Arbeits Kommando 91/382. (Eppink)

Another refusal of entry had ended in tragedy in 1942. A coach arrived with seven commandos under the escort of the security services. Eggers, the security officer, wrote in his diary: "7 October 1942. The so-called 'Norwegian Commandos' arrived at Colditz. We had no order from OKW to accept them and Colonel Glaesche refused to allow them into the camp."

Registered in the camp they would have been under the protection of the Wehrmacht (German army) and Protecting Power. Unregistered in the town jail they lasted less then a week. They were all shot. (see The Unseen Heroes.)

The lost commando of Colditz. Refused entry, they were accepted as prisoners at the Shooting House, which contained Dutch POWs. The officer with a white coat is a Serbian doctor. The man on the left is a camp barber and the man with an accordion is the camp cleaner. (Eppink)

• TWO •
THE GERMAN SECURITY BRANCH AND THE GUARDIANS OF COLDITZ

Captain Reinhold Eggers, the head of security from 1944 at Sonderlager Colditz, wrote to me in January 1970 on the work of his department. I've transcribed it verbatim. Some of his English is uncertain, but what it contains is fascinating:

"The German name for security is Abwehr, meaning the protection against danger from outside influences. The security officer was known as an Abwehr Officer or AO.

"We received secret instructions from the OKW to employ agents known as V-men or V-Manner, from 'Vertrauen' meaning 'to trust'. Unfortunately at Colditz we could not get any British V-men. I was like a cook without a kitchen.

"The only man to offer himself on his arrival was a Lt Purdy. Unfortunately my opposite number on the escape committee identified him within seventy-two hours and I had to lodge him outside the camp for his own safety. The only other was an orderly whose christian name was Douglas, I forget his surname. He was fed up serving officers and wanted to be moved to a stalag (OR camp). I made a proposal to him and he stood to attention and said, 'Captain, I am still English!' So I failed in my attempts.

"We of course were trained to listen carefully to remarks by prisoners and when one spoke in a superior manner with the 'imbecile Germans' we listened. One such case occurred when Neave and Luteyn escaped. We did not know how or when but guessed the park. The Commandant therefore forbade the park walk. A Dutch lieu-tenant approached me saying, 'It seems that the Commandant is thinking we are using the park for escaping, no! We have a way out that is always at our disposal.' I was relieved, now I knew I had to concentrate on the buildings. A small thing but this enabled us to find the hole under the stage. Talking had been dangerous and the mood of vain superiority too!

"I was confirmed in my conviction that the way out was inside the castle even by so keen and experienced an escapee as Mr Romilly. I met him running round the yard. He never did this up to then. He liked boxing. So I was astonished and asked him, 'Mr Romilly, what are you doing?' He proudly answered, 'I have to be fit if I am to have my turn for escaping!' He was so safe about it. What did this answer mean to me? Mr Romilly, as a Prominente, was under a special regime. He was free to move inside the castle as he liked, but he was forbidden to partic-ipate in the park walk. So it was absolutely certain to me that the way out was inside the castle.

"Later we had a special group of men that suddenly appeared and tried to surprise the PWs when they were busy making escape gear. We called the men (one NCO and three men) 'Rollkommando', a flying squad. These men supervised the Prominente controlling them, and the microphones, every two hours.

"Other duties of the AO were identity control (from time to time special identity roll calls were held). Then examining and improving the measure to hinder escapes: barbed wire fences, construction of special points for better observing the dead spaces between the dark corners of the castle (pagoda on the western terraces, wooden bridge for sentry no 9). Further, studying the tricks of the PWs that were to deceive the camp officers and sentries. Also measures for controlling the carriages that entered and left the POW yard (vehicles - bringing bread, laundry etc).

"A special activity of the AO was made necessary by transfers of PWs from Colditz to other camps and vice versa. The bad boys liked to organise impersonations of one nationality by another one, smuggling of information etc. Hiding places were gaps between teeth as well as the anus and bandages of false wounds. Securing

the transport against losses on its way was another task of the AO, also when PWs were sent for special treatment to hospitals. There, soon they were able to escape.

"Sabotage was another thing for the AO to look out for. Once, when the men fetched the kitchen scraps to feed their pigs, they found broken razorblades and glass in the waste. The poor pigs would die and so damage would be done to the German rations. Only the very massive reprisals [such as restricting the amount of food given to the prisoners] that the Commandant could think of put an end to this cruel kind of fighting the Germans.

"A routine action of the AO, repeated monthly, but irregularly, were the searches, sometimes on a large scale and by the 'help' of 'experienced' criminal commissioners from Dresden. Rarely did they bring a better result than the surprise ones of the camp officers, founded on patient observation. We never made a search without the presence of a PW as observer.

A report received from Vogt, the censor officer, by Eggers on the reverse of a postal form postmarked Colditz 7 August 1941. Translated into German, it is the second of two pages and therefore starts mid-sentence. It reads, "object found – and I did this three times and it causes me pain! EVERYWHERE and that they do not take them with the same courage as they did at the time, but are whinging and swearing like naughty children. Great! Have a go, RAF and Yankees, and think of 1940." Signed Peter. This is an attempt to stir up the Germans and talks of them being bombed. Below is written, "Whoever knows Capt Tunstall will know that this letter is only propaganda fiction and intended to provoke us." Signed Vogt.

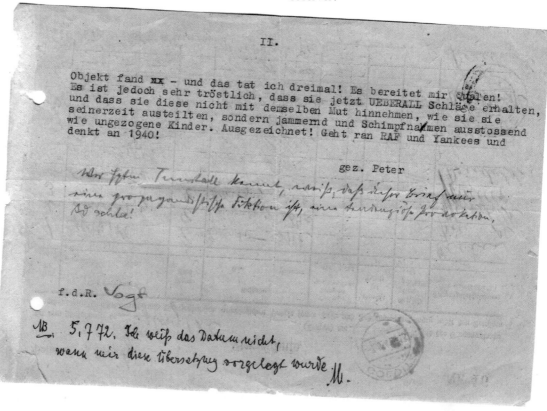

Censor office showing Sonderführer Kusel standing by the window reading a book. The photograph was received from Eggers with Kusel's signature on the reverse.

"Of course it was part of the duty of the AO to supervise letters, parcels, and books: in short the whole traffic between PWs and the outer world. This was the task of the postal department. It was under the care of Capt. Vent during the years of the war. Each letter was examined by heating it. Sometimes invisible writing appeared. If not, the letter was treated with a special chemical solution. If invisible words appeared the text was sent to the AO. Also lies about German matters were reported. Then the Commandant ordered the writer to be put under arrest for six to fourteen days. Officers' arrest was a solitary confinement with full kitchen rations. The 'Tiger', an old, pensioned criminal commissioner, was sent to Colditz to help the AO. His name was Teichert. He managed the arrests. In March 1942 the postal department discovered that in book boards contraband was smuggled into the camp (German money, maps for escapes, needles for compasses etc). The Commandant asked for an x-ray machine. It was soon installed. From this time every parcel was x-rayed. Contraband was confiscated. Sometimes

the monthly amount of money found in this way was about £100. Besides, these tools, compasses, maps etc. did not reach the customer. These items came from a Major Clayton-Hutton from a secret department of the War Ministry. Imitating this system of illegal communication the German OKW decided to organise this along the same lines. The Colditz AO, as the most experienced AO, got orders to pack about 100 parcels each month to German PWs. We took them to Torgau, the seat [headquarters] of some sections of the OKW. Our PWs in England, Canada, Australia etc had no chance to escape. Therefore we did not send money, tools and other escape material. The main contents were propaganda stuff: extracts from Adolf Hitler's speeches. Besides this we sent codes and a special plastic, called 'Phillip'. One could write by putting it over any pointed object. The words were invisible and could be made visible only by a secret chemical stuff. By this means we got secret news from our PWs; answers to questions we put to them. I was shown some answers. This whole system was an imitation of the secret communication between the British War Ministry with their PWs. It was called by the code name 'Unternehmen Ekkegard' (Enterprise Ekkegard); the rather careless British camp authorities never discovered it."

Eggers then gave a list of the staff of the security department, as follows: "Central office: the AO and one assistant officer with two clerks. Mail or postal office: one officer, up to a dozen interpreters for all languages, some sergeants and men for the control of parcels, keeping provisions and distributing the contents in no bigger rations than one daily. On the whole about twenty-five men.

"There was no supervision of the PWs. No wonder we were often outwitted by the selected activists called the 'bad boys!'"

Guard Duties

During World War Two, Defence Battalions 395 and 397 were responsible for the protection of the town of Colditz and acting on camp guard duties as required. 395 Battalion normally performed the latter chore.

Apart from Colditz Castle, there were two other camps in Colditz town. One, the Schützenhaus, was run as a conventional camp, but was designated a POW camp, as at the castle. The other was a slave labour camp.

Schützenhaus or Shooting House

This camp was located close to the edge of town. It consisted of a large single storey building set within its own grounds. Pre-war it had been a shooting club, the main form of entertainment in those parts. During the early years of the Nazi party the building was taken over as the local SS social and administration building.

Early in 1941 the OKW hired it as a recruitment camp for White Russians. Barbed wire was placed around the perimeter with a main entrance and guards from Batt. 395. On 1 June 1941 Eggers was promoted to captain and made the camp officer. There were about 150 officers present from the Polish, Yugoslav or French armies, they or their parents having left Russia after fighting the Bolsheviks in 1920. The camp was known as 'Schu' and administered by the castle camp. There were a few escapes by officers not wanting to fight for the Germans and in 1941 those who wanted to fight for the Germans against the Russians were moved to camps at Zietenhorst and Wutzetzt. In 1970 Onyszkiewicz told me that four Yugoslav officers of White

Photograph of the Dresden Pope with choir during a visit to the Shooting House. The Pope is reported to have been executed by the Russians because of this visit.

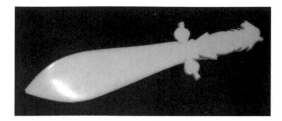

cers from the castle during the occasional purges by the security services from Berlin and Dresden.

In 1944 it was again reopened as a POW camp. On this occasion it held 'bad boys' from Holland who had not reported for work camps when required after they were released from POW camps. When they were found they ended up back in POW camps, a number going to Stalag IVB at Mühlberg. From there they were transferred to Colditz and lodged in the Shooting House, now known officially as Arbeits Kommando 91/382. It came under the administration of Mühlberg and had a Corporal Werppley in charge. The prisoners worked on the farms, in factories and mills.

Buchenwald Aussenkommando No 24 Colditz

This camp was sub-camp 24 of Buchenwald concentration camp. It was located in the Sektor Hentscke plant on the perimeter of Colditz. Hugo Schneider AG of Leipzig owned the factory. It was home to the large armaments firm HASAG. Under pressure from the Ministry of Armaments, concentration camp prisoners were permitted to be hired by HASAG as workers. The camp merely had to keep the numbers up to the required amount. The factory at Colditz had the code name 'C'. Hungarian, Polish and Czech intellectual Jews were held under the supervision of German convict Kapos (foremen), who impressed on the guards that they should be strict. The work consisted of producing panzer-fausts (anti-tank rocket launchers) and the dangerous task of installing detonators.

Guarded by SS of 4th Infantry Regiment SS Totenkopf Division, men unfit or educationally below standards who were not accepted into 1st–3rd Regiments were confined to guard duties. The Lagerführer was Master Sergeant Genz, a man with a pistol always at his waist and a whip in his hand. A sadistic murderer. Eggers reported that the SS guards had no association with Colditz Castle and lived in a village nearby in caravans similar to gypsy wagons. Opened in December 1944, the camp was evacuated on 13 April 1945 on a death march to Theresienstadt Ghetto.

Russian descent, who had refused to fight, were incorporated into the Polish contingent at Colditz after the camp was closed. Eggers informed me that he later learnt conditions were so bad at the camps his men had moved to, that he made representations on their behalf. This had little impact and most of the volunteers later died or were taken prisoner on the Eastern Front.

At the beginning of 1942 the Schützenhaus was made into a camp for Indians and Asians, known as an 'Indie' camp. Once again Eggers was put in charge of the daily routine. It was known as Colditz's bye-camp and continued to be administered by the castle camp. The prisoners worked in the earthenware workshop. Although Eggers said there was a happy atmosphere, the occasional escape still took place and on one occasion the prisoner on recapture stated he had escaped as there was not enough time to pray in the camp – he was a Muslim. By the end of the year it was decided to move the prisoners, the Indian officers being sent to Oflag 54 at Annaburg near Torgau.

The camp was then used to house the offi-

Bone paper opener made in the Shooting House by a White Russian prisoner and given as a gift to the Commandant, Captain Eggers.

A cup from the Shooting House used by a Polish prisoner in Colditz.

A request for a personal parcel sent to the Hollywood film actress Deanna Durbin. Written by a Serbian Lieutenant Krasnoff, a prisoner in the Shooting House.

A 'file' of watchmen at Colditz. Senior Sergeant Rothenberger, 'Franz Joseph', is seated at the front centre left with baton.

Sub Lt 'Dusty' Miller at Colditz wrote in 1983: "I have notes for 16 April 1945 which state at 4pm I went to see a Hungarian doctor just released from the concentration camp on the hill. In an American ambulance. Almost too weak to be interviewed. Ghastly condition. He whispered that the food was almost non-existent with a forced twelve-hour labour breaking stones that he could not comprehend [ie he couldn't understand what he was doing it for, which is justified as it was probably just a punishment]. I think his name was Nicholas Pullitzer and he was a chief surgeon in a Budapest hospital."

The SS camp commander received instructions to take the British officers of Colditz Castle with them when they evacuated.

Colditz Castle Oflag IVC

The guardians of Colditz Castle consisted of watchmen, Kommandantur and security staff.

Watchmen

These were taken from 4 Company of 395 Landisschufreu Battalion. Soldiers from this company were present until the end of the war. One of them, Peter Hofmann wrote: "From September 1942 until December 1943 I was at Oflag IVC. We had three files [squads] of about fifty men with an officer or senior sergeant. With fifteen sentries allocated to duties there were three men acting as relief. Working a 24-hour watch each sentry was on duty four times for two hours. The men lived within the castle area. File 1 was on the first floor facing the outer courtyard situated below the senior officer pris-

oners. Files 2 and 3 were in the old building named Krankenhaus in the road by the side of the park. My file leader was Lieutenant Strauss. The company leader was Captain Thomann. The 'Rollerkommando' or cycle-action group were also used for appells and for noisy occurrences or escapes. Sergeants Rothenberger, Gebhardt and Corporal Schadlich were used for this duty."

The duties of the watchmen were manning the guard's posts and entrances, and the guard paths and watch towers around the perimeter of the castle. In addition, as mentioned by Hofmann, there were cycle-action groups, ready in the event of an escape. Bicycles were the best mode of transport for the fields and heavy wooded areas around the town. As the war progressed a number of wounded soldiers returned from the eastern front were used as replacements.

Kommandantur

The administration of the castle was under the control of the Kommandantur. Under the command of the Commandant it consisted of the officers and also the civilians employed within the castle. Contract workers were also hired. Normal administration type offices also included the canteen and messes.

Security Staff

Those soldiers permitted within the prisoners' courtyard formed part of the Kommandantur security staff. Also included were the dog handlers, Prominente security team and soldiers involved in appells and 'action' groups. They were under the control of the head of security and senior Sergeant Gebhardt. It was policy where possible to change the manpower after six months to a year to avoid blackmail, bribery or corruption.

Colour photography at Colditz. Captain Kunz (adjutant) on right, at the approach to the Kommandantur. (*Hofmann*)

Guard house. Forty bunches of keys are listed in the key rack whilst fifty identity discs of the day are displayed in the cabinet.

Christmas celebrations for 1940 are held at the Wettiner Hof hotel, Colditz. Commandant Schmidt is seated at the end of the second table facing the camera. Also on the second table is Adjutant Kunz (facing camera fifth from right), whilst security officer Lange has his back to camera second from right.

Senior German officers at Colditz

Max Schmidt: a Saxon by birth he was one of the Old Prussian school, and described as a strict but fair officer. He inspected the camp more than any other Commandant, and was always at his desk by 8am when he inspected his staff. Anti-Hitler pre-war, he remained loyal on rejoining the army. He was a man who was very outspoken and once reduced a lieutenant to the ranks for dishonesty. He retired aged seventy.

Col Glaesche was Commandant from 1 August 1942 until 13 February 1943. Younger than his predecessor he was, according to Eggers, an ardent supporter of Hitler. Seldom seen inside the POW area, Eggers also stated that he ran the camp from behind his desk. Like Schmidt he was also insistent that his officers behaved correctly on and off duty. But for all that was said against him, he was in fact acknowledged for doing a great deal to improve security. His most important initiative was building the 'pagoda', a wooden tower on the garden terrace. Glaesche left to become a commander of a region in the Ukraine, being in charge of all POW camps. The original photograph shown of Glaesche (below right), given to me by Eggers, had been received post-war from Lange the photographer. As Colditz was in Eastern Germany any reference to the Nazi eagle or swastika had to be obliterated before going through the post. Eggers paid for these souvenirs by placing money into a West German bank and informing Lange how high a local lake had risen since he last wrote, which was his way of telling him the money was in the account.

Captain Priem was the camp officer from November 1939 until January 1943. A man reputed to have a sense of humour, a view not subscribed to by Solly Goldman! In January 1943 it was decided all officers should have a medical check to see if they were fit for duties on the eastern front. It came as a surprise to everyone that Priem was not only not fit for service in the east but that he was not fit for service at all; he was immediately retired. He returned to his hometown and took up his old post of schoolteacher, dying in his bed later that year.

Incidentally, Eggers told me that there had been two deaths of German soldiers in Colditz. The first was a corporal that took his own life in the office of Captain Vent, using his revolver. The reason was not known for the suicide.

He then handed me two photographs. This story, he said, was more serious:

"A young soldier of nineteen-years-old was found dead outside the parcels office. He had been shot with his own rifle. I investigated to find out the cause but there were a number of unanswered questions. The main one was that he should never have been in the prisoners' courtyard and certainly not alone. I discussed this with the Commandant. We could see the complica-

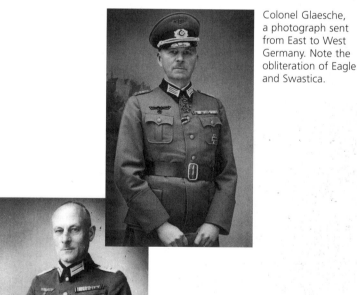

Colonel Glaesche, a photograph sent from East to West Germany. Note the obliteration of Eagle and Swastica.

Pagoda installed on instructions from Col Glaesche.

Colonel Schmidt.

Body of soldier found outside parcels office, an alleged suicide.

Below: A card dated 12 February 1941. Written by Col Schmidt to Frau Eggers to thank her for a reception she gave for the Colditz officers, it is signed by Col Max Schmidt (Commandant), Capt Kunz (adjutant), Capt Lessel (security), Capt Saurich (intelligence), Capt Priem (camp officer), Capt Kusel (censor), with endearment from Eggers. Eggers told me that the signature of Priem is the only one to his knowledge in circulation.

tions and decided we would leave it to the criminal police in Dresden. They came to the conclusion that there was no evidence of anything but suicide, which we accepted and the matter was closed. I have my theory!"

Colonel Gerhard Prawitt was Commandant of Colditz from 13 February 1943 to 16 April 1945.

Mrs Elizabeth Prawitt wrote to me of her husband's war years:

Lt Allan and Capt Priem. Allan always wore his kilt, unless escaping. When I asked in the 1970s what happened to the kilt he told me that he had not long thrown it away.

Original ID photo of Prawitt which he removed from the records.

Last letter written by Prawitt from Colditz.

The identity pass belonging to Prawitt.

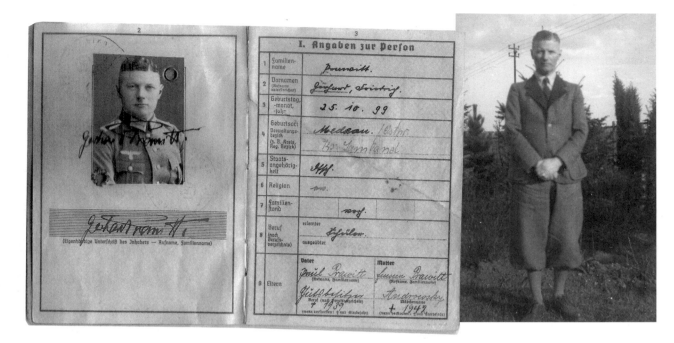

Above: Prawitt's pay book.

Above right: Prawitt in 1949 after release from Werl prison.

"My husband Gerhard and I were both born in East Prussia. I had a son Ulrich born in 1944 at Regensberg, where my husband was first stationed at the outbreak of war.

"He was a captain when he took part in the Poland campaign and later transferred to the French campaign. After recovering from being shot and wounded in the stomach he was sent to the Führer Reserve in Warsaw.

"In Warsaw the food at his camp was sabotaged and there was serious poisoning affecting everyone. Transferred to Strasbourg he was diagnosed as not being fit for active service. In December 1942 he was sent to Colditz where he was trained to take over from the Commandant Colonel Glaesche on 13 February 1943.

"My husband was held briefly by the Americans in a POW camp but on the safe return of the hostages [Prominente] he and the others were soon released. I was of course in Colditz and my home was in the eastern sector. The Russians would dearly love to have caught my husband. After his release by the Americans he stayed in an attic room at my sister's house in the western sector, I could not cross the border. Then he was tricked by two British officers he knew to go with them for a meal, when

this was over they said they were arresting him.

"Gerhard was not taken this time to a POW camp but to a prison for criminals at Werl. [This is where Kesslering and others accused of war crimes were held.] I learnt of him being there from a priest, three months after he had been captured, not knowing where he had disappeared and it was four months before he was released. Eventually I managed to get to the west and we were reunited.

"As for the film on Colditz, the producers tried to get Gerhard to cooperate and offered him big money. Even though the government would not allow him a pension, he still would not sell himself like some did and refused to help.

"Now I am the last of both officers of Colditz or their wives who is still alive. Elizabeth Prawitt."

Elizabeth Prawitt has since died.

Captain Reinhold Eggers (1891 – 1974), was at Colditz Castle between 1940 and 1945.

He was born at Halle in Germany in 1891. During World War One he served with distinction as a lieutenant in the First Regiment of Marine Infantry. He was awarded the Iron Cross

Eggers at Hohnstein, second from right.

Below: Despatch advising Eggers of his promotion to lieutenant and subsequent transfer to Colditz.

Bottom: Postal receipt from Colditz post office for the mail to be delivered to the Shooting House and signed by Eggers as Commandant.

2nd Class at Flanders on 8 May 1915, and the Iron Cross First Class and Hesse medal for bravery on the Somme in December 1916.

After the war Eggers was a schoolmaster. With an avid interest in the British schooling system he arranged an exchange between his school and one in Cheltenham. This proved very successful.

In 1934 Eggers gained a doctorate in philosophy with a paper on English education. The Nazi party had been elected and Eggers came under suspicion as he was not a party member and had encouraged further exchange of students. This was stopped and Eggers was permitted only to teach junior classes.

With the outbreak of World War Two Eggers was enlisted as a lieutenant in the Reserve Army and posted as an interpreter to the prisoner-of-war camp for officers numbered as Oflag IVA at Hohnstein.

He was assigned to escort duty for some senior prisoners being transferred

Right: Dress bayonet and scabbard belonging to Eggers.

Below: Copy of safe conduct pass written at Colditz 14 April 1945 and signed by Brigadier Davies (senior ranking officer), Lt Col Tod (Senior British Officer), and Col Duke (Senior American Officer). Copies had been given to Eggers and Prawitt, which proved to be worthless. This copy, belonging to Eggers, is the last to survive.

to another camp, and was permitted to have some home leave afterwards. On his return to Hohnstein he found the camp empty and in preparation for becoming a youth camp for bombed-out children. He then received orders for a transfer to Colditz Castle and promotion to full lieutenant as assistant to the camp officer Priem.

With his fluent knowledge of French and English, Eggers had a great deal of contact with the prisoners. Later, when the German officers were examined for duties in the east, Eggers was passed as fit for the Russian front. At the same time Priem was found unfit for service, so Eggers stepped into his job having been promoted to captain.

As the camp officer for the White Russians at the Shooting House, it was Eggers' responsibility to take charge of the mail received for his camp. Shown is a receipt for mail received at Colditz post office, the x's by uncollected mail was some for Eggers, which he has signed for using his Christian name.

In 1944 Eggers was placed in charge of security. His assistants were Senior Sergeant Gebhardt, whom Eggers suspected of assisting the prisoners and who was sent to the Russian front where he fell, and Corporal Schadlich, a very competent security man known as 'Dixon Hawk'.

The dress bayonet and scabbard came into my possession in the early sixties. As an honorary member of the Stalag IVB society I met an ex-prisoner who had been at Colditz. Knowing of my interest he brought this to me stating he had used it for chopping sticks and that he had relieved Eggers of it at the liberation. Years later when Eggers stayed at my house I showed him the bayonet. He recognised it but although I offered it back to him he thought it best it remained in the collection, as "he didn't know how much longer he had".

With the end of the war in Colditz the Americans made the German officers POWs. After a short period of time Eggers was released and returned to his hometown of Halle. Short of money he was more than pleased to be offered a job teaching a Russian officer how to speak English. However, when collected by a driver and escort for the first lesson he was placed under arrest as a 'war criminal'. There followed a period of interrogation until eventually he was

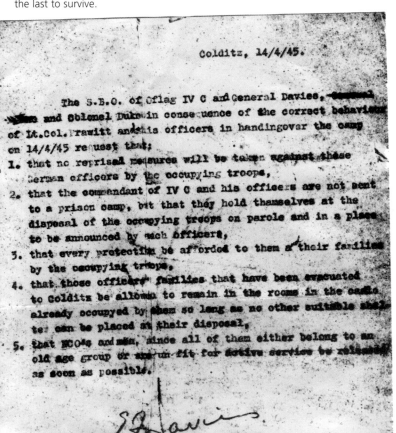

Colditz, 14/4/45.

The S.B.O. of Oflag IV C and General Davies, General and Colonel Duke in consequence of the correct behaviour of Lt.Col. Prawitt and his officers in handing over the camp on 14/4/45 request that:

1. that no reprisal measures will be taken against these German officers by the occupying troops,

2. that the commandant of IV C and his officers are not sent to a prison camp, but that they hold themselves at the disposal of the occupying troops on parole and in a place to be announced by such officers,

3. that every protection be afforded to them & their families by the occupying troops,

4. that those officers' families that have been evacuated to Colditz be allowed to remain in the rooms in the castle already occupied by them so long as no other suitable shelter can be placed at their disposal,

5. that NCOs and men, since all of them either belong to an old age group or are unfit for active service be released as soon as possible.

Letter written by Eggers from Torgau KGB prison.

found guilty of supporting the Fascist state and sentenced to ten years in a punishment camp. The year was 1946.

He spent the first six years in Sachsenhausen concentration camp. He stated that more prisoners died in that period than in the twelve years it had been under German control. This may be open to argument.

Whilst a guest in my home Eggers permitted me to tape an interview of his post-war experiences, which I have transcribed below.

"I was first allowed to write home in 1949. That was three years without a letter to or from home. What I sent was a card to say I was alive. I received one letter. [This was later given to the collection.] In 1952 they closed Sachsenhausen down, some prisoners were released but I had to complete my sentence and was sent to the KGB prison at Torgau. This was a true prison of retribution, run by the East Germans who had to prove themselves to their masters. To your question did I try to escape, no, I did not have the energy and suffered from TB. Three young lieutenants wanted to escape and asked my expert advice as I had been in charge of security at Colditz. I told them to plan. If they wanted a tunnel, then get material first. I told them not to go to the obvious place for the entrance and explained about the French tunnel. Have a fourth man to cover the entrance. Find somewhere close to the wall and under the wall and into the fire zone. We did not wear uniforms as they said we were criminals not soldiers, so they didn't have to trouble about civilian clothes. There was a tram stop outside the fire zone, we heard the trams. I collected money for them. The leader was from a Panzer unit, he went last to cover the entrance. The three escaped but the leader was caught in the fire zone. He was made to stand still all day long; if he moved at all he would be shot. He was given twenty-one days bread and water. They thought he was alone. The other two caught a tram and disappeared. The leader was sent afterwards to a punishment unit. Very few lived through being in the punishment unit but he survived and lives in Hamburg, his name is Bush. I was released in 1956 and banned from the Russian zone. I was allowed to write once to my wife from the prison and received one letter from her."

On release, he went into retirement and wrote the best-seller Colditz, The German Story.

• THREE •
THE ESCAPE COMMITTEE

On the arrival of the Laufen six at Colditz in November 1940, their first priority had been the organisation of escapes. They realised that they needed escaping equipment and proper documentation to travel across Germany. Outside help was required and the place to get this was from the War Office.

Code makers and breakers

None of the British officers at Colditz in 1940 had been versed in the official code. So instead Pat Reid and Rupert Barry decided in December 1940 to write a letter home using a simple code they had invented. Barry, knowing of his wife's ability with crosswords, was confident she would recognise and crack the code. Fortunately at that stage the German censor department were not geared up for cracking English codes, having only dealt with Poles. The Germans foolishly not only would have no dealings with the Polish officers but believed them to be a crushed nation, with no confidence left, who would not dare to oppose them by sending coded mail. This was a big mistake.

The Germans treated the British with a similar type of arrogance. An even bigger mistake. A code that would have been picked up immediately in 1942 was allowed to slip through the net at this earlier point. Reid never received a response to his letter to Ireland but Rupert Barry had better luck. The full text of his letter is shown here for the first time.

The code used is indicated by the first line "Am so glad to hear you are going to buy a puppy. The first dog in each three litters you will find the best!" This indicates that the first letter in each third word is the code. You can imagine that Rupert's wife at first thought he had 'wire fever' but soon realised the import. After help from a work colleague Mrs Barry eventually

Airey Neave, the first Britsh escapee from Colditz. Shown in the uniform of a German guard after a failed attempt.

managed to get Military Intelligence interested enough to take action. For those of you who wish to try and decipher the code I have left the secret text to the end of the chapter. A word of warning, Rupert was working under pressure and made a mistake early in the text. It also goes wrong at the very end, deliberate or otherwise is hard to tell. I am no expert and took under half an hour, with prior knowledge, of course, to work it out.

Gate to the terrace (on right), which Airey Neave successfully used to escape, whilst dressed as a German officer.

The letter (in protective plastic) written by Rupert Barry in code that started the official communication with MI9.

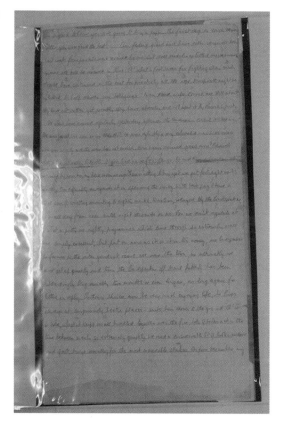

"Colditz, 6 December 1940.

Am so glad to hear you are going to buy a puppy. The first dog in each three litters you will find the best! Am feeling grand and have eaten very well today. Last week four parcels were received by me. Out of all Madeline's letters one was missing. However all will be received in time. Oh! What a fool I was for fighting when easily I could have continued in the east for practically all the war. Muspratt ought to be enlisted to help recover my belongings. Ivan and wife Connie are still about, they have not written yet, possibly they have already and not sent it by prisoners' post. All others have arrived regularly. Yesterday afternoon the American consul visited us. He was jovial. His son is in Aldershot. He was definitely a very educated man. Well Xmas will come slowly and the war has not ended. How many damned years more? Edward's letter sent not really legible. I have had no news of George. He and Edward Leagre will returned by now. Money here is amusing. There is nothing to buy yet we get forty-eight marks monthly. Our difficulty as regards it is spending the money. With back pay I have a total sum of something amounting to eighty marks. Wireless, relayed by the loudspeaker is on all day from noon until night descends on us. For we can't regulate it. What a pity as nightly programmes which come through so extremely well are simply excellent but put on now as it is too noisy, one loudspeaker performs in the outer yard – it roars all over the town so ultimately we must get up quickly and turn the loudspeaker off. Mail hither has been outstandingly long usually two months or even longer, as long again for letters in reply. Anthony should now be very much enjoying life, he lives always at surprisingly hectic places – suits him down to the ground. Oh! It is cold, in fact it keeps us all huddled together over the fire. Lots of books makes the time between meals go extremely quickly. We read a considerable lot of books indoors and if not, bridge usually for the most incredible stakes. As from December."

This is the end of the text (it seems to end mid-sentence) but the code must have ended before this as the last part does not make sense. Unfortunately the War Office was unable to assist with what they required as it involved the Americans

Two of the coded letters sent by the small team who had been taught the official code.

Coded letter received by the dentist Captain Green. Received in Marlag, it was sent by the Naval Intelligence Head of Department with the codename 'Outram'. Written in code it said, "important send circumstances of all losses our naval and merchant ships". Green was not permitted to use the code in Colditz.

whom they did not wish to compromise at that stage of the war. However, an unknown aunt wrote to Barry before he had an acknowledgement from his wife. He quickly assumed she was from Military Intelligence and on receipt of a further letter was able to translate that two parcels were on the way to two officers, whose names he received. Each parcel would contain separately a bag of smarties and a pack of handkerchiefs with different coloured borders. On receipt he had to place all the smarties of one colour in a bowl of water with a certain coloured border handkerchief. The official code was revealed on the handkerchiefs.

Rupert Barry was in charge of codes until the end of the war and he chose a small team of men to work with him at varying times during the years. Only the official British code writers were permitted to use codes at Colditz. This was difficult for Captain Julius Green, the dentist. He had had a successful liaison, passing code back and forth, from his days at the naval camp Marlag, with a young lady at Naval Intelligence who posed as his fiancée. The head of department posed as her father. A great deal of Naval Intelligence was exchanged successfully, but he was not permitted to continue this at Colditz. Only a certain number of people were allowed to send coded messages, to try and keep security tight, and Green was unfortunately not one of them.

Contact from Military Intelligence

The main source of contact at Military Intelligence with prisoners of war was MI9, located in room 166 at the War Office. As the war progressed their resources were stretched and the commanding officer, named Crockatt, was promoted to lieutenant colonel with similar promotion for his staff. The staff levels were then increased and they were allocated a house at Beaconsfield. His deputy was a captain named Winterbottom. Under him was the brilliant Clayton-Hutton who had little respect for authority and consequently was a bit of a maverick, but tolerated by those in charge because of his undoubted skills. Hutton was responsible for inventing 'gadgets' that were not only for prisoners of war and escape purposes but were also used for other 'undercover' activities.

The routine was that on receipt of a request via coded mail for material, Hutton if necessary would invent something to fit the bill, or supply from his stock. These would then be sent to G3 (Tech) which was under the control of Sergeant Ward. He organised the special parcels, known officially as 'phoney' parcels but by the prisoners as 'explosive' parcels.

A sample of the Indent Form is shown overleaf, which was a list of items requested to be sent to a prisoner in a parcel. Dated 14/10/41, it is for Captain Harry Elliott at Colditz. He was planning a 'hardarse' escape. However, Harry thought he was not fit enough for another term of outdoor activity. He therefore decided upon the fake repatriation escape, as related in a later chapter.

On one occasion C-H, as Hutton was known, received a list of one hundred names to which phoney parcels were to be sent. From that list twenty-three were at Colditz with a further eight who were destined for Colditz, two of whom were to be Senior British Officers.

When MI9 first started, C-H read all that had been written on POW camps of World War One. He also interviewed returning POWs,

particularly escapees. The first RAF escapee was Flt Lt Harold Burton, later to retire as an air chief marshal. Captured on 6 September 1940 he eventually arrived at Luft I. When in solitary confinement after having been captured whilst involved in building a tunnel, he found that the bars of the windows were merely screwed on. It took him two days to work them loose and make good his escape. Arriving in Sweden on 31 May 1941 he was awarded the DSO and Military Intelligence used him for lecturing aircrews. A report on his experiences had been sent under cover to C-H at MI9 with a covering letter from his father attached. Hutton was delighted to receive this and used Burton's experience for his gadgets.

In contrast Captain Winterbottom had received a letter from Goodyear of the War Office. This gave information from a World War One POW on the handling of parcels by the Germans at that time. Acknowledged by Winterbottom it was sent to C-H who stated on the bottom in red-pencil that, "Burton and Sholto Douglas gave a different view. This is 1941!"

Presents from MI9

It was an unwritten law that the Red Cross was never to be used for any purpose that may be detrimental to the organisation. This did not mean that the string or twine used to secure parcels from them was not used for different purposes! Military Intelligence and MI9 in particular needed addresses of convenience, to use as a cover for sending material. Two well-known organisations at Colditz were the Licensed Victualler's Sports Association of EC4 and the British Local Ladies' Comforts Society of Victoria Street SW1. The latter was one of the main sources of 'explosive parcels' received by the prolific escapee Benji Stewart-Walker whose activities had landed him in Colditz. Shown opposite is a sample label from an 'explosive parcel' he received.

The most common escaping aids received by the prisoners were maps, followed by money and compasses. It did not take too long for the Germans to discover most of the methods used to transport these objects. When items continued

Indent for the phoney parcel for Capt Harry Elliott.

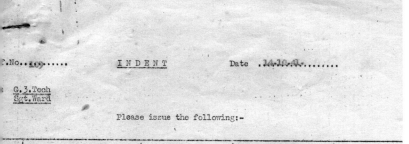

SPE/4/1047

SECRET

The War Office,
Room 373,
Hobart House,
Grosvenor Place,
LONDON, S.W.1.

VICtoria 1244/226

2 Sep 41

Dear Leslie

You may be interested yourself and will probably like to pass on to Clayton Hutton the following experiences of Col.Binnie (of Permit Branch) when a prisoner in the last war:-

"In most camps, when parcels arrived they were opened in front of us on a counter. We had very little opportunity of seeing the outside of the parcels and certainly it would have been difficult for us to see whether or not they were post-marked in a particular way. After the parcel had been opened we saw the contents. Tinned food was not the first place, instead a label with a number was stuck the tins were stored. When we wanted the tins we went to the Germans opened and examined the tins emptying the con which we took away. Actually in most camps we managed to many tins unopened out of the Store. Books arriving in pa not handed over to us in the first place but were kept to handed over to us later. Only clothes were handed to us ov None of the outside wrapper of the parcel was ever given t

Of course it is possible that different arrang force during the present war. I actually received a consid of articles hidden in tins. As I knew what kind of tin the packed in I always managed to smuggle them out of the Stor I got consisted of German money in jam tins, maps, a compa tools which could be used for escaping, including an insul I suppose altogether I got as many as 50 tins with contrab

Capt. L. Winterbottom,
M.I.9b.,
Room 166,
War Office.

Yours ever

Leonard

BRITISH LOCAL LADIES COMFORTS SOCIETY

Lt. B.S.Walker,
British Prisoner of War 1144,
Oflag IX A/H, Germany.

112 VICTORIA STREET, LONDON, S.W.1

Left: Letter from Goodyear to Winterbottom with comments in red pencil by Clayton-Hutton.

Below: List of one hundred names for phoney parcels. Apart from the names for Oflag IVC (Colditz), men who were later to be sent to Colditz are also shown – Tod who was to become SBO at Colditz (Oflag VB), Broomhall (another future SBO), Ginn (Oflag VIIIC), and Colt (Oflag VIID).

Below left: Sample label from an explosive parcel, received by Stewart-Walker.

PARCELS LIST "B"

Names taken from "Parcels List".

CAMP	NAME	P/W.No.	PARCEL TYPE	DATE OF DESPATCH
OFLAG IVC	2/Lt. A.M. Allan	10511		
	Major W.F. Anderson	478		
	Capt. R.R.F.T. Barry	480		
	2/Lt. H.E. Barton	536		
	2/Lt. J.R. Boustead	15656		
	2/Lt. A.R. Campbell	223		
	Subt/Lt.(A) A. Cheetham R.N.	1265		
	Sub/Lt.(a) J.M.P. Davies R.N.	158		
	F/O M.W. Donaldson, R.A.F.	336		
	Capt. H.A.V. Elliott	258		
	Lt. T.H. Elliott	1155		
	P/O F.D. Flinn, R.A.F.	1267		
	P/O. N. Forbes, R.A.F.	2257		
	Lt. E.G.P. Harrison	11854		
	Capt. J.C. Hobling, C.F.	1118		
	P/O F.D. Middleton, R.A.F.	335		
	S/Ldr. B. Paddon, R.A.F.	1121		
	Lt. P.S. Pugh	238		
	F/O. G.F.A. Skelton, R.A.F.	600		
	F/O. D.S. Thom, R.A.F.	585		
	P/O. H.D. Wardle, R.A.F.	208		
	Lt. R.J. Hyde-Thomson	482		
	Lt. Comdr. O.S. Stevinson	1282		
OFLAG VB	Lt. R.K. Archer	204		
	Major E.J.A.H. Brush	1043		
	2/Lt. P.N. Elgood	407		
	Lt. P.F. Hanbury	564		
	Capt. C.H. Keenlyside	300		
	Capt. B.H. Mytton	1562		
	2/Lt. H.B. Robinson	925		
	2/Lt. R. Steele-Mortimer	920		
	2/Lt. M.P.S. Truell	1093		
	2/Lt. P.F. Sedgeley	1568		
	2/Lt. J. Caven	507		
	Lt.Col. W. Tod	1554		
	Capt. H. Westley	663		
OFLAG VIIC	Lt.Col. E.H. Allen	474		
	Lt.Col. W.M. Broomhall	916		
	Capt. A.H.S. Coombe-Tennant	506		
	2/Lt. F. Crouch	244		
	Lt. R.W.N. Danielsen	524		
	2/Lt. C.N. Janson	574		
	Lt.Col. J.C. Mackay	1117		
	Capt. E.A.F. Macpherson	1341		
	2/Lt. A. McCall	813		
	Lt.Col. E.K. Page	1255		
	2/Lt. J.C. Robertson	684		
	Lt.Col. R.B.Y. Simpson	364		
	Major T. Stallard	368		
	Lt.Col. H.R. Swinburn	1253		
	Capt. B.D.S. Ginn	1323		
	Major F.L. Trotter	865		
OFLAG VIID	2/Lt. H.W. Ashton	474		
	2/Lt. R.H.D. Colt	237		
	Lt. P.J. McCall	629		

Above: Selection of maps received at Colditz from MI9. The maps show the borders of Bulgaria, Belgium, Hungary, France and Switzerland, with most important the crossing at Schaffhausen, a popular destination for escapees.

Right: Photograph of Cenek Chalupka, the man responsible for bribery and corruption. A Czech RAF sergeant, he posed as an officer.

to get through before the parcels had been examined, by burglary (they overrode the alarm system) or snatched by distracting the guard, then the Germans finally realised that the parcels office could not remain within the prisoners' courtyard. Consequently, from 1944 very few items sent by MI9 came into the possession of the escaping committee. However, they had sufficient supplies of material sent already. In addition they knew that under the superb control of the Czech pilot Chalupka they could get what they wanted by bribery, corruption and blackmail. But finally, after the massacre of the fifty from Luft III, escaping was not encouraged because of the executions and veiled threat contained within a leaflet circulated to all POW camps that escaping was no longer a sport, see opposite. Lives could not be risked with the war drawing to a close.

Maps, money and passes

In the early days before the Germans became aware of the methods of smuggling used by MI9, a wealth of material was received by the prisoners. This arrived in games of all descriptions, books using the spine and boards, or records that were peeled apart.

In addition to these methods, which were mainly used for transporting maps, labels on tins and double thickness tins were used to hide money. This method was stopped when the contents of tinned food had to be emptied into a container in the presence of the Germans. Moreover, the Germans refused permission for tins to be received after the discovery of the French tunnel, when a large number of tins were found having been joined together for air to be pumped through for ventilation purposes.

As far as maps were concerned, the escapees preferred their own brief plans showing the main routes and towns they needed to pass through, in addition to a detailed plan of any borders.

Playing card maps were also popular. The fifty-two cards when peeled apart revealed a complete map of Germany with the joker as the key. One card is a souvenir of Dick Howe, the escape officer. An American sergeant found the

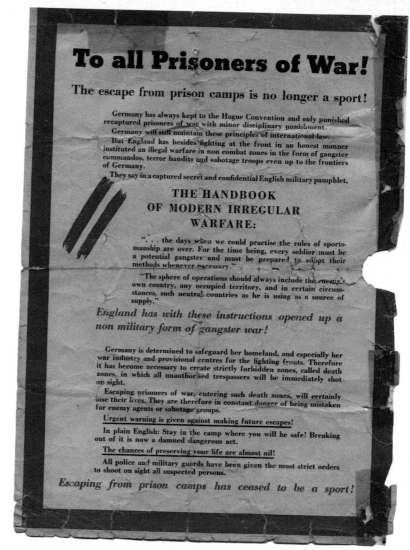

peeled card on liberation day, lying in the prisoners' yard (see page 48). As the war progressed all aircrew carried an escape kit that included a silk map. I am told evaders mainly used them.

Displayed on the Colditz noticeboard by Eggers, who later removed it.

Passes

Forged passports and headed notepaper were useful documents received from MI9, but passes were normally made at Colditz. Originals were 'borrowed' from one of Chalupka's contacts, or purchased or stolen at any opportune moment. Skilled forgers, like Ken Lee, would prepare travel permits, leaving the date blank to be inserted at the time of escape. Completing the text in indelible pencil obtained from the canteen, they could then make copies of the documents by pressing the item onto a slab of prepared jelly.

Two cigarette packets containing money. Found in the Colditz hide, one has the name of the Canadian escapee Vandalac written in pencil.

Right: Escape was not an adventure. This is illustrated by the treatment received by Colditz officers Milne, Middleton and Storie-Pugh after recapture. This memorandum originated from the American Embassy in Berlin which was responsible for the British Commonwealth prisoners' welfare at that time. It was sent to the Foreign Office who forwarded it to the War Office and MI9.

Below: Parcels office at Colditz with food tins being opened.

The following extract from a memorandum received by the Foreign Office from the American Embassy in Berlin will interest you:-

STRICTLY CONFIDENTIAL

"Berlin W.8
Wilhelmstr.   74/76.

"The Foreign Office has the honor, in reply to the Memorandum of February 10 - Nr.536 - concerning the British Prisoners of War, Officer Milne and others, to inform the Embassy of the United States that the investigation by the appropriate authorities has resulted in the following:-

"The captive British Flight Officers Milne and Middleton attempted to escape August 21st last year; they were re-captured by the guardians sent after them only at night in a forest during a very heavy rain so that a certain excitement reflecting against the captives on the part of the guardians is understandable. A sub-Lieutenant, who struck one of the officers, has been punished.

"The British captive Lieutenant Pugh had also attempted to escape. He got as far as the railroad tracks after darkness where he tried to jump on a passing train; at this moment he was arrested by an inhabitant of the town Bergheim. The captives were kept in an inn until the guards arrived, where they were allowed to sit at a common table. During the transport back some of the guards did not act towards the captives according to regulations; they were punished accordingly by the camp commander. Lt. Pugh and also the man of confidence for the English Officers declared their satisfaction thereby.

"It is assumed that the aforementioned cases may be considered settled".

Photograph of tinned food recovered by security staff. Right to left are: Captain Lange (security officer), Captain Vent (post officer), Mr Teichert, the 'Tiger' (retired criminal investigator), Corporal Paschinski (drawer of plans), Gefreiter Klingst (Eggers' clerk), unknown, unknown. Paschinksi drew the plans of the French escape tunnel.

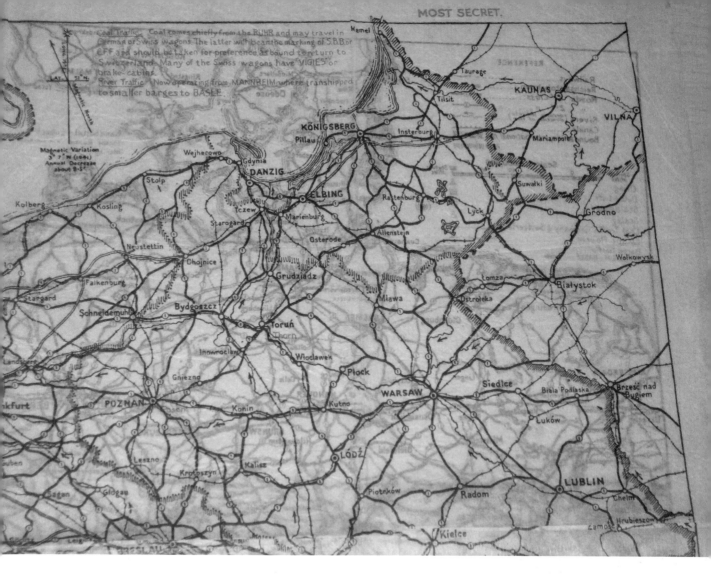

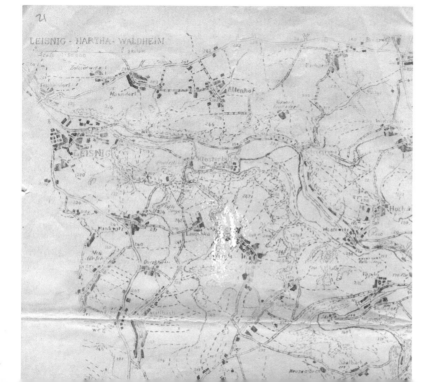

Above: Map marked 'Most Secret' with escape routes from named POW camps and escaping advice.

Left: Master map used for copying onto a jelly mould.

Playing card maps and fake ID.

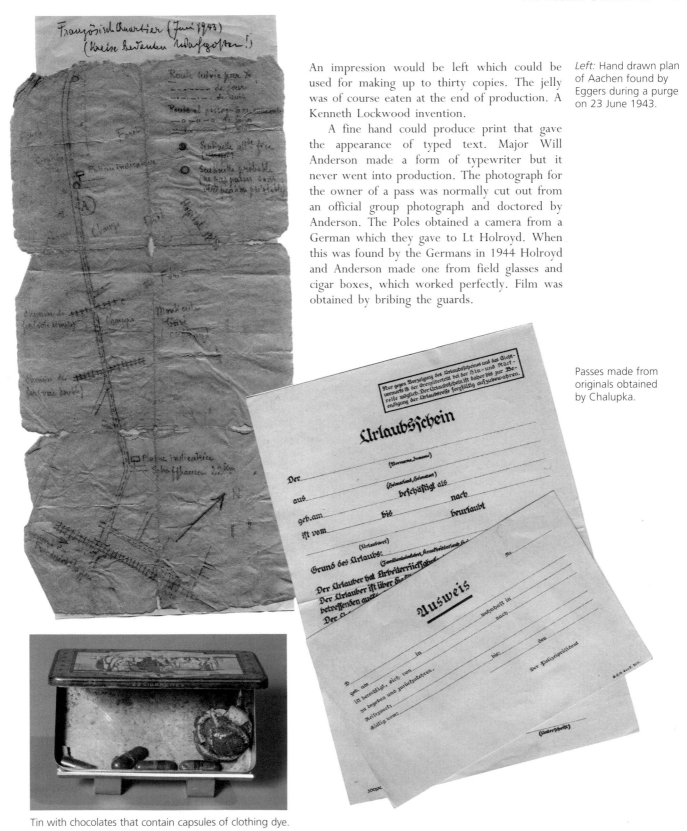

An impression would be left which could be used for making up to thirty copies. The jelly was of course eaten at the end of production. A Kenneth Lockwood invention.

A fine hand could produce print that gave the appearance of typed text. Major Will Anderson made a form of typewriter but it never went into production. The photograph for the owner of a pass was normally cut out from an official group photograph and doctored by Anderson. The Poles obtained a camera from a German which they gave to Lt Holroyd. When this was found by the Germans in 1944 Holroyd and Anderson made one from field glasses and cigar boxes, which worked perfectly. Film was obtained by bribing the guards.

Left: Hand drawn plan of Aachen found by Eggers during a purge on 23 June 1943.

Passes made from originals obtained by Chalupka.

Tin with chocolates that contain capsules of clothing dye.

Clothing

An exchange of clothing between nationalities could provide useful additions for civilian attire. Royal naval jackets and RAF trousers were always popular. Blankets of certain colours received from family parcels in England were also useful, and sometimes requested from MI9. Theft of headware from unsuspecting German workers was another supply. Dyes made from indelible pencil lead were used, but where possible capsules of dye from MI9 were highly sought after. One method was to send capsules enclosed in a box of chocolates, unfortunately discovered by Eggers.

The tools used for clothing alterations were primitive until a wooden sewing machine was made. This was strictly under the control of the escape committee for making German uniforms. Major Anderson with Lts Harrison and O'Hara were the main tailors.

Compasses

RAF prisoners arriving at Colditz sometimes had compasses with them issued as part of their escape kit. These came in the form of collar studs, buttons etc. Other basic direction finders were made from magnetised pieces of razor blades, or metal penholders that had been magnetised by a loudspeaker magnet. MI9 smuggled compasses in a wide variety of ways, the favourite being the fountain pen. The Australian RAF officer 'Bush' Parker, who was an excellent magician with amazing sleight-of-hand skills (used many times to fool the guards), was mainly responsible for producing homemade compasses.

Forged keys

Bush Parker with his many skills was also a master of forging keys and made all those required for escapes by the British.

Razor blades

These were the most precious and common commodity used for escapes at Colditz. With every window having iron bars hundreds of razor blades were needed for an escape where windows were involved.

Escaping aids

There follows the story of one escape where tools were used to help smooth the way: the canteen tunnel escape.

Kenneth Lockwood was canteen officer when in January 1941 a tunnel was begun from the

Exact replica of the sewing machine in Colditz Museum, used in the BBC series.

Real or fake?

FURTHER INFORMATION:
The BBC television drama series 'Colditz' ran for 28 episodes between October 1972 and April 1974. Although not always historically accurate, it helped to renew popular interest in Colditz. Copies were made of some of the prisoners' escape aids to use as props during the filming. They were made from similar materials and by similar methods, so it is sometimes difficult to tell the difference between the original items and the replicas. All the items in this showcase are replica props used in the BBC series. Try comparing them with original objects displayed in the other showcases.

241

Above: Pen compass used by the ERAs Lister and Hammond in their home run escape, and a button compass.

Left: Crucible lock and key bits together with a key, made by van Doornick.

Below left: Soap used for key impressions.

Below: The prisoners' canteen from where the tunnel escape was made. Kenneth Lockwood is seated on the far left with Charles Lockett standing fourth from left. This photograph was posted exactly a year after the escape, from Lockett to his wife.

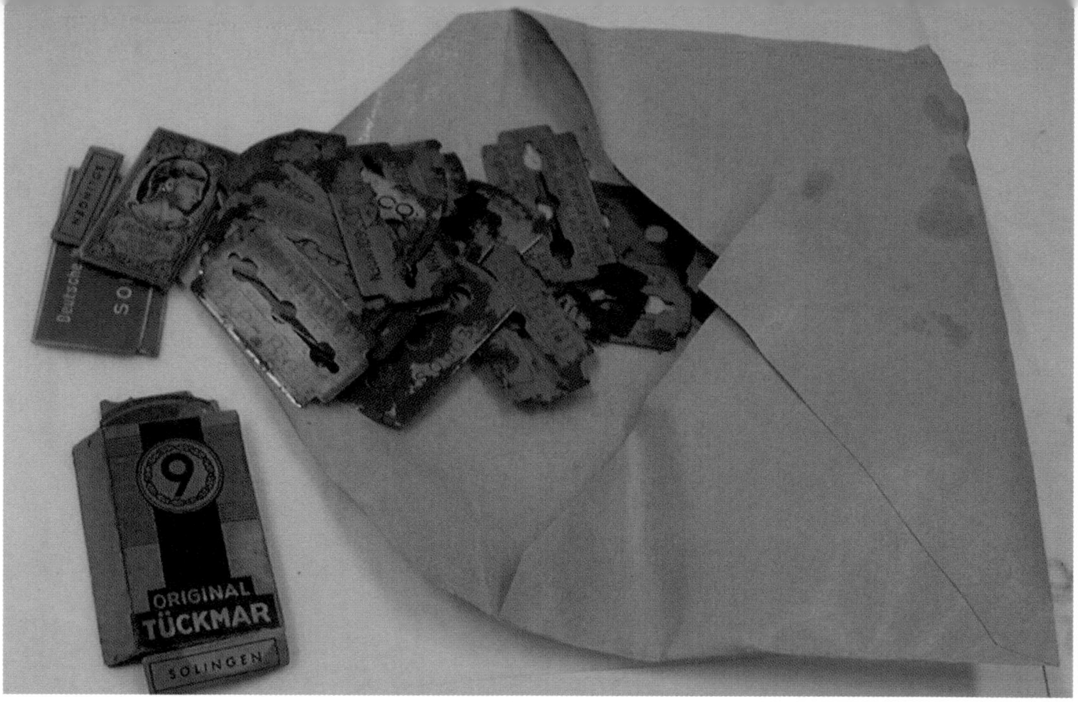

Selection of razor blades used for cutting bars at Colditz.

canteen. Pat Reid had hoped that a drain tunnel in the centre of the floor had access outside the castle to the stream in the park below. On examination however he found it did not even breach the canteen. But they had the basis for the start of a tunnel and the project began.

A German was always present when the canteen was open and Kenneth did not have access to the keys. However it was simple for him to 'borrow' them from behind the counter

for duplication purposes. Entry would only be able to be made at night and a four-month operation begun. Twelve officers including the Senior British Officer Colonel German were involved in the operation. 29 May was chosen as the date to open the tunnel onto the terrace above the park. Guard Post 9 controlled this area and it was vital to obtain his co-operation. A bribe was arranged and accepted. But the guard reported it to the Commandant.

Eggers wrote in his diary:

"29 May 1941. The British had tried to bribe one of the sentries by giving him 100 Deutsch Marks with a promise of a further 600 if he would close his eyes at a certain

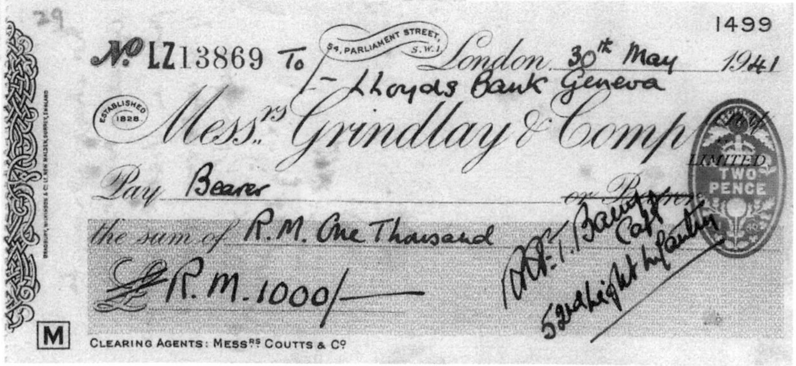

Cheque prepared by Rupert Barry for the canteen tunnel escape, to be used as a bribe.

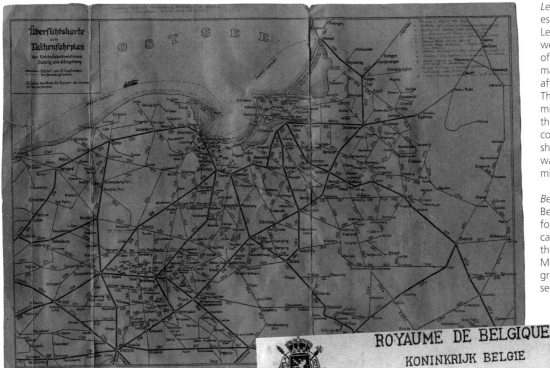

Left: The rules of escape by Squadron Leader Paddon. These were written on one of a pair of tram maps sent to Colditz after his home run. They were written minutely in pencil in the top right hand corner of the map shown. An extra rule was found in the middle at the top.

Below: Forged Belgian identity card for Barry to use in the canteen escape under the name of van der Meulen. The photograph was taken secretly.

time. Unfortunately for the British our man was loyal and reported the matter to our security branch. All the necessary details of the escape plan were known to us and Captain Priem with some soldiers was waiting. Captain P. Reid, eleven British, and two Poles were discovered plus an enormous amount of food. As a result we took security measures with regard to the food parcels and allowed the prisoners a little at a time and the remainder was kept in the stores."

Rupert Barry was number two out of the tunnel, following Pat Reid with whom he was due to travel. Intending to travel as a Belgian worker, Barry had an impressive Belgian identity card. The photograph in a dark jumper was taken in a corner of the castle. Should they reach a border and be challenged by a guard then Barry had made out a cheque on his Grindlay and Comp. account for one thousand Reich Marks payable in Geneva and dated 30 May 1941. It was endorsed on the reverse, "This cheque can only be cashed by Messrs Lloyds of

Geneva on special instructions by me and Messrs Grindlay's of Parliament St. Signed RRPT Barry 52nd Light Infantry. British Army."

In 1944 Col Tod instigated a major overhaul of security and the escape committee itself. His main priority had changed and he now had to prepare for the defence of his men when the need arose in the closing stages of the war. He was well aware of the SS presence in the local concentration camp and the very real threat to the well being and lives of the prisoners.

In 1972 Dick Howe, the escape officer, wrote about the part he took on the committee:

"For three and a half years I was in charge of all escaping under four Senior British Officers – Guy German, 'Daddy' Stayner, 'Tubby' Broomhall (for a very short period) and Willie Tod. I took on the job after the escape of Airey Neave and I made a deal with Guy German that I would not escape myself until ten British officers had made a home run. It was a sort of benevolent dictatorship, aided by such sterling characters as 'Lulu' Lawton (my first mate), Kenneth Lockwood (in charge of money and maps), 'Bush' Parker (the ace lockpicker), 'Rex' Harrison (the chief tailor), 'Checko' Chalupka (bribery and corruption), Ralph Holroyd (photography), Grismond Davies-Scourfield (the chief 'stooge'), Jacques Houard? (a professional forger), and many others who were continually on call for a variety of activities. I have put a question mark after Jacques Houard's name, as this was a nom-de-plume, which he used, as he was one of the world's leading stamp forgers in peacetime!

"There was no such thing as a committee other than taking note of all the various degrees of expertise one had available from the team who were responsible for any particular action, such as bar cutting by Lulu Lawton and 'Bricky' Forbes. They would tell me how they would like to do a particularly difficult job and I would see that they got every assistance in the form of diversions (Peter Storie-Pugh and Peter Tunstall), tools ('Scarlet' O'Hara), etc.

"Every man had a set of false documents made out for him, which were held by Kenneth Lockwood, in case he needed them for a snap escape, together with maps, money, concentrated food and railway timetables. Such was the anonymity of this team that on various occasions, when I have met Eggers in this country, he confesses to having no idea I was the main thorn in his flesh along with the others he regarded as 'good' prisoners, with the exception of Peter Tunstall who, by virtue of his speciality of creating noise diversions at my behest, spent the best part of 400 days in solitary confinement.

"I had a splendid liaison with the French (Lt. Guigues) and the Dutch (Capt. Van den Heuvel) and I still see Guigues fairly frequently. In my view Guigues was the best and most complete escaper I have ever met, as he was highly intelligent and fearless, an expert lockpicker and forger and he had the facility of disappearing into thin air, which I found most intriguing. When he left Colditz, he bequeathed to me the most ingenious radio installation, a method of getting into the German parcel office and many other helpful devices.

"The Poles were under threat to their families but Lt Just did not seem to mind about these reprisals and was very active.

"Did Colditz therefore live up to its reputation as the 'escapers' camp? The answer to this must be a resounding 'Yes'."

Every camp had its unique escapes, some resulting in the participants ending up in Colditz. There may have been more home runs in other camps, for example Luft III. But Colditz was the only camp dedicated to escaping and accepting the reprisals as a consequence, even if all the prisoners were not all directly involved as potential escapees. Schemes were hatched within the castle; often on how to get out officially, then make their escape and the number of attempts made for all nationalities was well into three figures.

The number of home run escapes from the castle were five British, involving eight POWs, four Dutch involving six POWs, and three French involving three POWs.

Dick Howe continues: "The final question is 'How did the escaping activities affect the prisoners at Colditz?' For those who were actively involved either as escapees or 'stooges', it gave them a purpose in a mundane existence and helped pass the time. At the beginning, in a multi-national camp, then there was a question of national honour. The competition to have a home run was very serious, so much so that in the early months there was a sense of mistrust between the nations and their plans were kept secret. It was not until the Paddon incident of the 'lady's watch' (page 103) that the escape officers realised co-operation was necessary, resulting in multi-national escapes and a 'common enemy'."

Those that made a home run of course had freedom and subsequent awards. They never forgot their comrades left behind and made every effort on their behalf. Paddon, an experienced escapee, went so far as to note some advice on the front of one of a pair of tram routes sent to Colditz by MI9 (see page 53). It is written in pencil in tiny capitals, making it extremely hard to read, even with a magnifying glass. The advice consisted of:

1. Route\Best by rail
2. English W\Parties in __?__ good value
3. Route via Kreuz and Komtz best
4. No control of passes via Kreuz
5. Control on special via Marienburg. Avoid
6. Brown pass ok at Kreuz
7. Leave pass essential if travelling via Posen
8. Watch Danzig central control, Gestapo in evidence
9. French are suspect in Danzig
10. Slow trains do not stop at Stargard
11. Police patrols at Dansk harbour difficult. Avoid if poss
12. Large W\Parties in Stetin will help if contacted

There is also a thirteenth 'rule of escape' which was at the top of the map away from the other rules. It is not clear exactly what it refers to. It says: "Work permits thoroughly checked at Danzig. Watch signature. Beets and lees ok."

Recaptured escapees and those who sacrificed their freedom in planned 'goon baiting', to help break the morale of the German sentries or as part of an escape, literally 'paid' an extra price. Being confined to solitary confinement meant that during the period inside you received no pay.

The camp paymaster, Lt Cdr 'Mike' Moran, kept a very precise account of the POWs pay and issued a pay book. 'Errol' Flinn, an intrepid escapee, has one page of deductions with running total, shown as:

Cells	Dates		Pay Deductions	
Camp	**From**	**To**	**R.M**	**Total**
Oflag IVC	28.8.41	23.9.41	43.20	43.20
	2.3.42	30.3.42	44.80	88.00
	4.4.42	2.5.42	44.80	132.80
	5.5.42	2.6.42	44.80	177.60
	21.8.42	24.8.42	5.20	182.80
	18.5.43	28.5.43	18.00	200.80

It was therefore a costly business for the likes of Hunter, Flinn and Tunstall and those other POWs too numerous to mention who notched up hours of 'solitary'.

A burning question – were they ever reimbursed by the British Government or did they treat it like the worthless (as it was only usable in the camp) lagergeld forced on the prisoners?

The Rupert Barry Code

"Get from War Office American Pasport Visa Ex Sweden In Germany for Switserland France Spain Portugal, Hotel Labels Stockholm."

This is the translated code I obtained, spelling errors and all.

A selection of lagergeld, the 'money' given to the prisoners, used in Colditz.

Sun-Pat

6ᴰ Milk Chocolate 6

RAISI

MAYPO

Such

HEINZ
POTATO SA

MADE FROM POTATOES, VEGETABLE OIL
SUGAR MUSTARD SALT, CHIVES, TRAGACANTH

READY TO
SERVE

IN SERVED AS HORS
LETTUCE AS

HEINZ
TOMATO
SAUCE

57

• FOUR •
FOOD FOR THOUGHT

Major Neale arrived at Colditz in June 1943 as a recaptured prisoner involved in the 'Eichstätt tunnel', one of the largest escapes of World War Two. He had been one of the leaders of a team of five, and number seven of sixty-five to leave the tunnel.

These are his thoughts on food at Colditz, written in two long letters in 1969.

"14 November 1969. At Colditz we had mess rooms and a certain limited kitchen space, apart from our sleeping quarters. After escaping activities or study of one sort of another, the main preoccupation of every POW was food – planning, rationing and cooking to make the Red Cross food which supplemented our meagre German rations go as far as possible.

"For most of the time at Colditz I was custodian, menu planner and head cook for our mess of about twenty-five/thirty officers. As generally we would go to bed hungry and wake up ravenous this was a very exacting task. We had a 'sofa' in our room made from Red Cross boxes and stuffed with dried vegetable, which I believe, was a residue from the soya beet factories. We thought it was so nauseous that even in hunger we could not stomach it but we never gave anything back to the Hun for fear he would cut the rations; most messes flushed it down the lavatory. We made the sofa. Towards the end when things were really bad we cut open the sofa and ate the stuff!

"Incidentally, regarding Red Cross parcels. I am told that very few went astray in Germany but that there was a considerable amount of pilfering at the docks, more in fact than in transit in Germany.

"28 November 1969. You asked how many rooms for a mess of thirty, one room, with three-tier bunks you can get thirty/thirty-five men into a room 20'x 20' or even smaller. As for a typical menu, there was no such thing. It

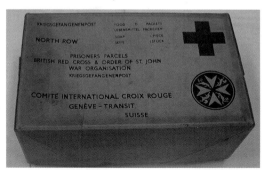

An original British Red Cross sample box with contents.

57

depended so much upon the availability of Red Cross food to supplement our diet. Note the bread ration did not vary much during the whole time I was a POW, it was 1/5th of a loaf per day, about five thin slices. A British doctor who was a specialist in dietary requirements estimated this to be the minimum needed to keep an aged invalid alive.

"We had British Red Cross parcels, ones from Canada and some from our gallant allies 'down under'. After the Americans came into the war we had some American food parcels too but not in addition, it was a question of one or the other. The British Red Cross arranged distribution of all parcels.

Dutch menu for Christmas 1942 signed by captains of the Royal Military Academy including Boogh, Elders, Nowens, Bijvoet, and van Nimwegen.

We were never allowed to keep unopened tins, so most messes drew only what they considered necessary for the week and left the balance in the 'tin store' to be drawn at some future date. Weeks and months might go by with no parcels so the proper build up of the tin store was the greatest responsibility of the mess food supervisor. Some POWs never joined a mess; a few just gorged what food was issued as it came in, some formed messes of two, four or eight people. In my experience the larger messes with twenty/thirty people were able to arrange a balanced 'menu' to the best advantage. But it depended to a large extent upon the cooking facilities available in our rooms as distinct from those of the German cookhouse, which was mainly devoted to the preparation of the food the Hun issued. Tea from Red Cross parcels was generally pooled and stewed up and issued from the German cook house, naturally under the strict supervision of the British member of the cook house staff. Mostly we drank it neat, perhaps with a little saccharin or sugar, never with fresh milk. Except for a very brief period when we had a little skimmed milk, the only milk, dried, condensed or evaporated came from Red Cross parcels.

"The supplementary items, sugar, margarine, jam and tea from the German rations were so small in quantity that they could almost be negative from a dietary point of view. We did get a small amount of so called dripping, fat, call it what you like. We called it 'man fat' from the rumours that the inmates of the concentration camps supplemented the Hun fat ration. I think it was horse fat. We did not eat it unless we were very hungry indeed but with a floating wick it made good fuel for little fat lamps to read or play chess during the switch off of power during air raids.

"A typical breakfast would be: tea or coffee from our Red Cross parcels (after used as warm water for shaving), two-three slices of German bread with enough Red Cross margarine or butter to spread thinly,

German canteen.

Dutch officer invited to British tea party. Watercolour by John Watton. This appeared in the book *Detour*.

a little jam or paste followed by a cigarette to calm any pangs of hunger. The black bread of Europe, Roggenbrot, and the rather sour tasting rye bread, was the only bread I tasted for 5 years.

"Midday: the German issue of soup, mostly if you could have strained this I doubt whether an ounce of solid matter would have been found. Also about half the daily potato ration, often 25% inedible, a slice of bread and a piece of Red Cross cheese.

"Evening: we left our small ration of fuel for cooking for the evening when most messes or individuals had the main meal of the day. There was no possibility of personal cooking of food. Any food which had to be heated was just put into a container of some sort labelled with the mess number and the duty cook put it in the oven on the top of the stove and when it appeared reasonably hot shouted 'mess 10, your grub is ready'. The evening meal might be: a slice of corned beef or spam or any other Red

Cross meat mashed up with the remainder of the Hun potato ration, flavoured with a marmite cube perhaps bulked with a few ground up biscuits, put into a Klim tin (we had no conventional cooking utensils) or if you were lucky a mess tin and served up moderately hot with the remaining slice of bread, a cup of cocoa, no milk or sugar unless you were lucky and then the pudding or cake. Well known to Arctic explorers, men in the trenches in 1914-18, and seamen, in fact everywhere where bread and flour was non-existent, the crushed biscuit flavoured with dried fruit, milk powder, cocoa and bulked up with as much water as possible without making it too soggy was a great favourite as a filler of the stomach, for a short time at least.

"I think the greatest lack we suffered was in the quantity of bread, potatoes etc needed to fill the stomach. The Hun rations by themselves were quite inadequate, the Red Cross supplies bridged the gap from a nutritional point of view and most certainly saved us from the malnutrition effects suffered by PWs in Japanese hands, as we always felt hungry.

"There are times I can remember of officers at Colditz queuing before the cook house for the peelings of turnips to scrape what extra they could obtain from them. A disgusting horse's head boiled to provide soup, left by the bin outside the cook house to humiliate us, barrels of Sauerkraut so rotten that the smell from the unopened barrels could be smelt throughout the camp etc.

"Memory however tends to be kind and it is easier to remember the more amusing episodes. As to the rest, it is difficult to explain to those who were not there that they ever happened at all."

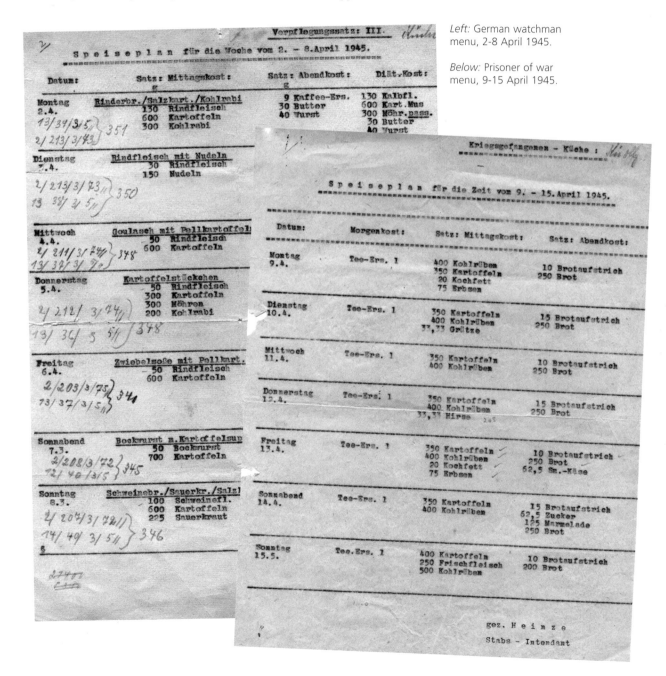

Left: German watchman menu, 2-8 April 1945.

Below: Prisoner of war menu, 9-15 April 1945.

• FIVE •

TUNNEL FROM THE SKY

At the beginning of March 1941 a meeting took place at Colditz Castle of the French escape committee. Chaired by the senior French officer (Brigante), accompanied by the escape officer (Guigues), two officers were present to propose an escape plan. The following account represents what could have taken place.

The small group of French officers sat at the trestle table in the centre of the long room.

There were wooden bunk beds lining the thick stone walls, with daylight just filtering through the small deeply recessed barred windows. The occupants were huddled in close conversation, a haze of smoke hanging above their heads.

"Gentlemen," the senior officer rapped the table with his knuckles. There was a respectful silence. "Let us begin."

With that he turned to the escape officer seated beside him who looked in turn at the figure guarding the open door. He received a nod indicating the area was free of German guards. This officer then walked from the room closing the door behind him. He took up his position in the narrow passageway at the top of the winding stone steps. Leaning over the stair rail he looked down the three flights that led to the entrance of the block. On each landing stood a lookout and two large men sat on the step to the entrance arch, casually reading books and blocking any entry.

The group within the French quarters turned their attention to the two men seated at the end of the table, who had kept a respectful silence during the preceding exchange of words.

Looking at the slimmer of the pair the escape officer opened the proceedings.

"You say you have a plan which will allow the French contingent, who so wish, to escape as one group?" Pausing he then added, "If successful, is that correct?"

"Yes," was the reply received.

"Very well lieutenant, kindly explain to the committee the plan you have in mind."

The officer glanced around the table and then with a half smile said: "It is a tunnel," then waited for the negative response he expected. He was not disappointed.

"A tunnel, from where?" an elderly officer asked with disdain in his voice. "Do you not think that the Poles and British, besides our own men, have not already explored every avenue possible for a tunnel route?"

The young lieutenant's companion, a thickset officer, joined in the conversation.

"Where, sir, would a tunnel normally begin?" the officer asked.

The elderly officer was no fool and realised he was falling into a trap but replied warily, "A tunnel means underground, therefore it starts at the lowest point."

Knowing of the proposed plan the escape officer expected and heard a smart answer.

"Exactly, but our tunnel will start at the highest point."

"I see," the major replied, "a tunnel from the sky eh!" He smiled at his companions. He was rewarded with polite laughter.

Waiting for the laughter to subside the escape officer instructed, "Tell us your plan."

The slim lieutenant took up the narrative.

Inside the chapel during a church service for prisoners of war.

"The entrance will start from this room." This received a brief buzz of conversation before he continued, "Or to be precise through that wall," pointing to the end of the room.

"As you all know, the clock tower is beyond that. We also know that this has a sleeve where the rope for the bell is located. There is a recess on each floor for the purpose of inspecting the rope; each recess has a door as access to the sleeve. The one for this floor is beyond that wall." Once again he pointed at the wall.

"How wide is this sleeve?" the elderly major asked.

The lieutenant glanced at his companion before he replied, "That may be the problem. We suspect it is not that wide and intend to explore before we give an answer. The rope will assist in the descent and ascent of course."

"Thank you," the escape officer said. "There is also the possibility of a tunnel a couple of centuries old leading from the castle. It is my opinion and that of the General that this is worth

an exploration. Your opinions please gentlemen."

There was a lot of discussion and in the end it was decided to explore further.

Diary of Reinhold Eggers, 18 March 1941: "Lts Paille and Cazamayou - French - apprehended whilst tunnelling in the tower of the chapel. It was then that Captain Lange [security officer] gave the order that all doors, which lead from the different floors of the castle into the tower, be walled up."

Cpl Schadlich of the security section in fact found the French officers. In addition Lange had the bell rope and chains removed.

Eggers wrote: "Special locks and padlocks were fitted to the attic door leading to the clock tower. The security locks had crucible cylinders."

This was only a temporary setback for the French, as they managed to obtain crucible locks.

Jean Brejoux, the 'father' of the tunnel, wrote in March 1973:

"The famous tunnel. The attic entered this on the fourth floor through a secret trapdoor in the floor. One descended the clock tower by making a hole through all the ceilings. All the doors giving to the floors had been walled up by the Germans, as there had been an earlier attempt to use the tunnel at this point and drop down into the cellar.

"From there we pushed a hole through the wall hoping to find a sort of crypt under the chapel – but without success. We then sawed the beams under the flagstones in order to creep down to the foundation of the chapel and thence to the foot of one of the castle towers. Here we made a vertical well down to below the foundations (encasing it with planks) and then set out along the horizontal gallery in the direction of a small separate tower quite close to some barbed wire. From there we thought that we would come out into the park. The tunnel was, in fact, discovered just as we had reached the small tower – by the adjutant, with the nickname Mussolini (whom he resembled a little).

"At that moment I was on the second floor in the little hall where, with two of my fellow POWs, we were repairing sacks to be used for clearing away debris, stones and earth. Mussolini had to get a young fifteen-year-old lad, who was slim enough, to go down the clock-weight channel which reached the second floor (we had already swum through to that point). When the poor lad saw three unattractive hairy men in the semi-darkness, he became scared, but I reassured him at once.

"In order to affect our escape we had to stave in the brick partition separating us from the bathroom. A Belgian major called de Liedekerke who was having a bath at the time was amazed to see us appear through the partition. Nobody had seen us and we had time to get back into our normal gear in time for roll call. From that time on the Germans realised that the tunnel was the work of an international team and they demanded that we should all pay for the damage.

"To dispose of the debris we had twenty POWs whom I detailed every evening to different points. We discharged the loads of debris into a large attic along the side of the roofing – moreover we had worked eight months in day

Access from bell tower to rope sleeve.

Access from clock tower to wine cellar.

Access from wine cellar to chapel illustrating the bags and pulley used to remove debris. Air tube made from Klim tins can be seen to the left of the entrance.

and night shifts. The sketch of the tunnel drawn by the Germans corresponds very closely to the real thing, except that there are no outlets into the floors. I believe the tunnel was forty-five metres long."

As mentioned Staff Sergeant 'Mussolini' Gebhardt of the security staff found the entrance, when he entered the clock tower with a civilian

Gap available to crawl beneath the chapel floor.

electrician Poehnert and his apprentice Reinhert. They were there to do work in the tower and whilst this was in progress Gebhardt idly opened the trapdoor of the rope sleeve, the rope having been removed on the orders of Lange. Shining his torch down he wondered why his powerful light did not go down beyond the third floor. Dropping a piece of clock mechanism it made a loud noise, striking a wooden cover wedge across the sleeve. Gebhardt was suspicious and lowered Reinhert on a fire hose. He sprung into action when the youth shouted out that three prisoners were in the recess.

Racing out, Gebhardt raised the alarm, whilst running for the third floor barrack room. The prisoners in the meantime had smashed through the recess room and escaped via the bathroom before the guards arrived.

The Germans found a hole had been chipped away in the recess to the floor below and so on to the ground floor. There a tunnel had been cut through the airshaft that ran at a steep angle, which the French had hoped would lead into a crypt. Instead they found themselves in the wine cellar.

Edgar Duquet, vice-president of the French Colditz ex-escapees club wrote in 1975:

"Having spent two stretches in Colditz I worked on the tunnel with the support team. The first team, having started from the roof, had already left the cellar when I joined it. Brejoux and Madin were the main men who helped on that part of the tunnel. They were keen from the outset and devoted themselves to the operation for about six months."

One of the main problems faced, and one that threatened to stop the tunnel excavation, was a large boulder that could not be moved, as there were not the tools available for the job. The British in the form of Dick Howe then came to the rescue. Francis Flinn, a RAF officer who was a 'keen type' for escaping as his solitary confinement record confirms, had made an audacious theft of a crowbar. This happened simply after a civilian worker had left his tool unguarded in the prisoners' courtyard. Francis ran forward and grabbed it; a guard saw this and gave chase as Francis ran up the prisoners' staircase, and the jemmy went from hand to hand then to disappear. It was delivered to the French who were able to dislodge the boulder. Flinn was given a place on the tunnel escape list, the only non-Frenchman to appear. Dick Howe was given a personal tour of the tunnel; the only Tommy's helmet available was handed to him to wear. He described the tunnel as 'amazing'.

Reinhold Eggers' diary. 16 January 1942:

"I was called to the cellar and when I arrived I found there was rubble everywhere and on a platform was a trunk filled with escape material. After a further search one of the soldiers loosened a stone in the wall and there to our delight the tunnel opened out and travelled for fifty yards in the direction of the park side of the hill upon which the castle is built. It so happened

The final stage where the shaft is dropped to the tunnel towards the small outer tower. Also illustrated is the method of lighting used during the dig.

French menu dated 5 September 1942 illustrating the clock tower and chapel.

that at the same time this was going on, the Gauleiter of Saxony, Herr Mutschmann, was paying us a visit and was quite amazed at the activities of our prisoners. Of course the staff were much relieved at the result of my searches."

Finding the tunnel was a great triumph for the German security department. They all received extra leave from the Commandant. In addition Corporal Paschinski, a member of the team, was instructed by the Commandant to draw a plan of the tunnel.

Eggers wrote to me that on 14 April 1945 he went to the Colditz Museum to destroy the most important escaping equipment/sensitive material, on instructions from Command. "The tunnel plan was on my list but fortunately I did not have time to destroy it."

In post-war years there was some controversy regarding Airey Neave's book in which it is alleged that the Commandant's wine was replaced with urine by the tunnelers as they were going through the cellar.

After Eggers had complained to him of an interview he gave to the magazine *Bild*, Airey Neave wrote to the widow of the Commandant, Colonel Prawitt. In fact, Prawitt had not been present at Colditz during the tunnel escape and alleged replacing of the wine with urine, so it hadn't happened while he was at Colditz. Frau Prawitt thought it of little consequence, and that it was probably a joke or misinformation.

Reinhold Eggers, in a letter I received in 1973, wrote:

"What a nonsense! Prawitt was not at Colditz before January 1943. I cannot even remember bottles being in the wine cellar, they were empty stacks. I often controlled the cellar. There were bottles there in 1939 and some in 1940 but they were for sale to the POWs for special occasions like birthdays. These bottles were bought for the canteen and stored there. Bottles for our mess were never stored in the camp and it certainly became rare in 1941 when the paymaster took the last from the canteen. I shall write to Neave."

From: Airey Neave, DSO, MC, MP.

HOUSE OF COMMONS
LONDON SW1A OAA

11th June 1974.

Dear Frau Prawitt

Thank you **very** much for your letter of the 12th May.

I have now heard from Dr. Eggers that the story of the wine cellar in Colditz could not possibly have occurred during your husband's time there, and that it was certainly not his cellar. The incident, which I heard about from another Officer, must have occurred before he became Kommandant. I am glad, therefore, that the story amused you and caused you no distress.

It was very kind of you to write.

Yours sincerely
Airey Neave

Frau Elisabeth Prawitt,
Kerschensteinerstr. 1,
241, Molln/Luneburg,
Federal Republic of Germany.

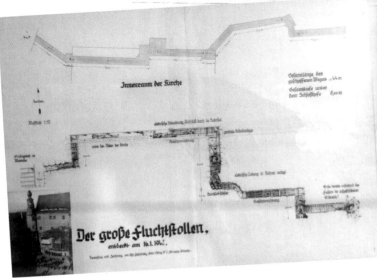

Above: Letter written by Airey Neave in reply to a report in the German press, which is attached to the letter.

Left: The original plan drawn by German security of the French tunnel.

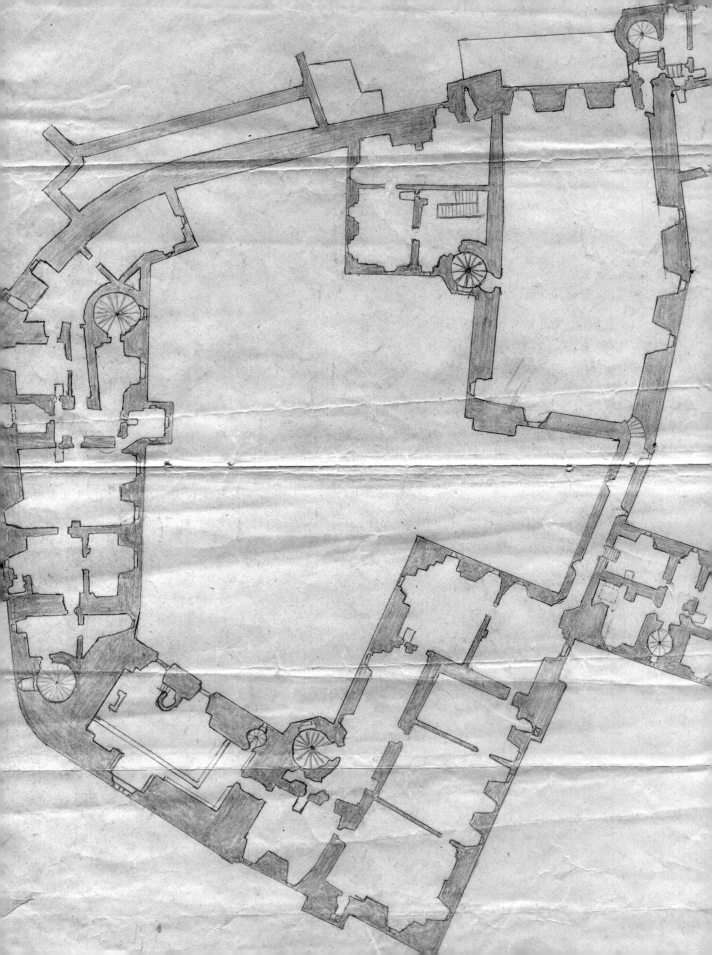

• SIX •
THE PLANS OF COLDITZ CASTLE

Reinhold Eggers and I were seated at a table in my home discussing tales of Colditz from his period as security officer of the castle. I brought up the subject of the Countess and the suggestion that a tunnel had been built from her castle to Colditz Castle for liaisons. Eggers thought it was merely a legend but one the British believed might have been true, resulting in the prisoners attempting to obtain plans of the castle, which they managed to do very successfully. He spoke in mock horror. We laughed and then becoming more serious he added, "We laugh now Michael, but believe me it was no joke when my security staff brought me the plans after a snap raid."

With that Eggers opened his briefcase and extracted a folder containing three sheets of paper. They looked slightly aged. As he laid them on the table I immediately recognised them as the floor plans of the castle. One sheet had pinholes in each corner.

"Here," he gathered the sheets together and handed them to me, "you now have the plans of the castle for your collection." We then spoke of other things.

My research into the plans showed they were of more use to the prisoners than Eggers ever realised. The British used them, together with other information they received, as a basis for building a master plan of the castle. This was to prove of immense importance for the escape committee when discussing an escape plan.

The receipt of the plans was due to three people: Lt Peter Storie-Pugh, a persistent escapee held in Colditz, his father Major Pugh, a veterinary surgeon and Commander of the Police Specials in West Kent, and thirdly Captain Winterbottom of MI9, the man responsible for military intelligence between London and Colditz.

I received an invitation to visit Major Pugh at his home and once settled in his charming bungalow he showed me a number of letters on the subject which he allowed me to copy.

In January 1941 he had received a letter from his son Peter in Colditz. This was in code, the key letter of which referred to his son's schooldays. The coded information was naturally passed through to Captain Winterbottom at military intelligence.

In August 1942 Major Pugh received a letter from Captain Winterbottom:

"Here is a pretty problem! The 'boys' want to have plans of the Schloss at Colditz to show, if possible, any underground passages and or 'priest holes'. In this connection historical gossip links the Countess of Rocklitz as having had an affair with the owner of the castle and is said to have made use of an underground passage from her own castle to that of Colditz, sometimes known as 'Alt Fursten Haus'.

One of the three plans (ground floor) received from MI9 of the castle.

"It is possible that the British Museum might be able to produce some plans and I was wondering whether you would have time sometime to go there and see if they had anything about the Schloss."

27.8.42, Captain Winterbottom from Major Pugh:

"The chaps appear to think of you as the masculine counterpart of universal aunts. The story of the naughty Countess of Rocklitz certainly seems interesting and I will waste no time in trying to find out if there is any evidence of the existence of this passage. Frankly I believe many of these stories are concocted for the interest of visitors and probably increase with the telling. It certainly would be great if one could discover something to send out in answer to their request."

9.9.42 Winterbottom to Major Pugh:

"We have been informed that there is a book in the British Museum by Bellger, which gives a historical description of the town of Colditz. The book was published in Leipzig in 1832."

Pugh went to the library of the British Museum to look for the book without success. However, the elderly keeper who knew the book collection well was able to produce a different book about Colditz Castle in which were copies of plans of the castle (architect's plans). A photostat was made and forwarded to Winterbottom.

7.10.42. Winterbottom to Major Pugh:

"Many thanks for the photostat copies. We are extremely grateful to you for your help and will work on them."

Letter from Sqd Ldr Paddon, an escapee from Colditz, to Major Pugh. Paddon had sent letters to many of the POWs once he had made his home run:

"11.11.42. RAF Helensburgh. Dunbartonshire. Dear Major,

Many thanks for your letter. As you can imagine I have been snowed under with replies to my circular.

"I should be very interested to know from where you obtained the detailed plan you mentioned, as it is exactly what I suggested to our mutual friends, and added suggestions as to where to get it.

"Peter has more than a chance because he is one who ALWAYS keeps on trying."

As a postscript to the account of the plans I received a letter in September 1974 from Jock Hamilton-Bailey, who organised the Warburg Wire Job escape:

"I certainly did use a copy of the plans you have for a base for my map. It showed of course only the ancient fort of the castle, but using these as a starting point I was able to build up the rest, by intersecting sight with a sight rule on a homemade plane table. Thus I was able to plot in the more modern part of the buildings, including nearby houses (but roof plans only of course) and also the positions of sentry towers etc., and flood lights. When taking sight I never had the complete plan on my plane table, only a blank sheet with the minimum marks, so that if caught nothing much was lost. The details were then transferred to the main plan in secure conditions."

It is from the plans sent to Colditz by MI9, as found by Eggers, that all finished products which appear in books were produced. Unfortunately for Eggers as the prisoners had built up a master copy, it was not really much of a hindrance to them when Eggers found the map.

Peter Storie-Pugh drawn by Watton. His father obtained the Colditz plans.

SEVEN

PAT REID – MR COLDITZ

Patrick Robert Reid, a Captain in the Royal Army Service Corps, was captured on 27 May 1940, after the defence of Dunkirk. Having been given a 'capture card' to post to a close relative, giving details of his capture, he arrived ten days later at his permanent camp. This was Oflag VIIC at Laufen. A large brick building, it had once been the ancient palace of the Archbishop of Salzburg. Pat soon made contact with like-minded officers and started excavation of an escape tunnel.

Only two teams of three were considered a safe number for the actual escape. Two of the original selected had to drop out although one eventually made a home run and the other ended up in Colditz. On 5 September 1940, with the new replacements the tunnel was opened and the escape took place. Two officers, Pat Reid and Kenneth Lockwood, used a temporary disguise of exiting as women. This escape constituted the first tunnel escape by British officers in World War Two.

Unfortunately both groups were captured within ten days and returned to Laufen where they were placed in cells awaiting court-martial. This never took place and instead they were given varying lengths of solitary confinement. Pat was given a month, the longest sentence of them all. However, none of the escapees served the full period for they were released and after ten days were told to gather their belongings as they were leaving the camp. On 10 November 1940 the group, having travelled by train under escort, arrived at Colditz. They were the first six British Army officers incarcerated there and were known as the Laufen six.

Shortly after their arrival they were joined by Lt Col Guy German who was made SBO and in January 1941 having made 'escaping the order

of the day' he elected Pat Reid as escape officer.

The escape officer was of course forbidden to escape and therefore in April 1942 Reid decided his time had come and asked to be released from his position. Dick Howe took over. Pat could now plan his own escape.

Billy Stephens and Ronnie Littledale put forward a rehash of an escape always thought too risky, asking Pat to join them. Although originally not enthusiastic about the route because of the high risk, he nevertheless agreed. As

Capture card issued to Pat Reid on 30 May 1940, three days after being taken prisoner.

From left to right: Onyszkiewicz, Pat Reid, Bartoszewicz, Peter Allan, Karpf.

Colditz 1941. From left to right: Pat Reid (Big X), Peter Allan (toilet escape), Jim Rogers (secret radio), van Rood (Czech pilot), John Watton (Colditz artist), 'Lulu' Lawton (escape committee), 'Pop' Olver (died in captivity), Dickie Barton, and Colin MacKenzie (code writer).

Exit shaft from cellar where Pat Reid and his fellow escapees, having removed one bar and their clothes, managed to escape.

Stephens and Littledale had planned to travel together, Hank Wardle was offered a position as Pat's partner, which was accepted. This made the escape a cross service effort with one Navy, one RAF and two Army officers involved.

On 14 October 1942 the four made their exit from the kitchen window, having bent back one of the bars, and crossed the rooftops from the prisoners' to the Germans' yard. The escape was nearly aborted, as they found the intended door, with access to an outside window, could not be opened. They then found a cellar and on investigation saw a narrow ventilation shaft protected by two bars, high in the wall of the cellar. On being lifted up, Pat saw that it led to the outside terrace. The shaft though was too narrow and protected by the bars. Once again the alternatives were discussed and an abort considered. Pat decided to see how secure the bars were before making a final decision.

He found that the cement on one bar was crumbling and after a difficult struggle for both Pat and the person holding him, the bar was

eventually removed. There was still the problem of the width of the shaft but desperate men called for desperate measures and they stripped off their clothes and after a considerable time, bloodied and with torn flesh they squeezed onto the terrace outside the castle. It was 4am on 15 October 1942.

Travelling as a Flemish workman Pat carried amongst his documentation a letter of invitation to visit his girlfriend near the Swiss frontier.

Written by a French officer it reads:

"Belfort 28 September '42

"My darling,

"I am very happy to hear that you've finally got leave and that you think you will be able to see me.

"Here, lots of work, but we usually have Sunday free. It gave me a lot of pleasure to receive your letter, even though I will not be able to see a lot of you during the week. Never mind, we can go together to see my mother at Coliver on Sunday.

"The work at the Post Office is very interesting, and I am very happy here, at Belfort; but not as much as when we were together. Do you also remember, my darling, those tender moments that we shared?

"How is it that you have managed to get a job in the region? It will be so nice to be close to each other. I missed you a lot, you know!

"See you soon my sweet. I kiss you tenderly on your darling lips.

"Yours,

"Jeanette"

Illustration carried by Pat Reid in his escape. 1942. Seen on 'This is Your Life' programme on 14 February 1973.

After many adventures all four crossed the Swiss border. Pat and Hank surrendered to a Swiss police officer. It was 8pm, 20 October 1942.

It was important to let them know at Colditz that a home run had been made, for morale.

Luzern. Bahnhof und Pilatus (2132 m. ü. M.)

The 'Murgatroyd' card sent to Colditz by Pat Reid and Hank Wardle after their successful escape and arrival in Switzerland.

Back and front of card sent by Pat Reid to his mother in Kent after arriving in Switzerland. It appropriately illustrates bears in a cage of which he writes, "not like these bears any more."

John Mills, who took the part of Pat Reid, with his family on the set of *The Colditz Story*.

Above: A signed photograph of Pat Reid with David McCallum at Pat's first return to Colditz since the war. The visit, made in 1972, was for the BBC television *Colditz* series, in which McCallum played a leading role.

Left: Card sent by Pat Reid to his aunt after his arrival in Switzerland. His aunt wrote at the top "posted by Pat after escape".

Below: Card sent by Hank Wardle to Rupert Barry (in charge of codes) at Colditz. Posted on the first anniversary of their arrival in Switzerland. Hank mentioned being entertained by O'Toole (by which name Rupert knew Pat in Colditz).

Right: Programme for the premier of the film *The Colditz Story* signed by John Mills. Shown in the presence of Princess Alice.

Below: Veterans on the set of *The Colditz Story*. Shown from left to right are: Dick Howe, Peter Allan, Padre Platt, Jock Hamilton-Bailey, Pat Reid, unknown, unknown. At front, from left to right: Ivan Foxwell (producer), John Mills, Guy Hamilton (director) and Lionel Jeffries.

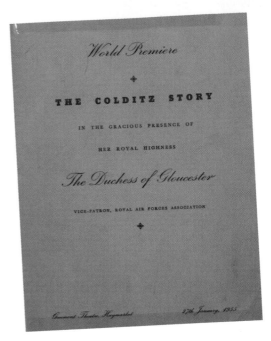

Pat Reid accompanied by Gerald Glaister (producer of *Colditz* series), with Brian Degas (creator of series) behind Pat, being stopped by 'the man in the trilby', Eamonn Andrews, for 'This is Your Life'.

Consequently, three days later Pat wrote the following card ending with a heavy P written by Pat and a heavy H by Hank. Addressed to the code officer Rupert Barry it read:

"23.11.42.

"This is to wish you and all your friends a very happy Christmas and all the luck in the world for the New Year. You've no idea how sorry we are that you are not with us. Things are moving fast these days. Give our dear love to your friend Dick [Howe]. We are having a holiday here.

Love from Harriott & Phyllis Murgatroyd."

Murgatroyd was a pantomime name and one by which Hank Wardle was known by Rupert Barry.

Whilst in Switzerland Pat Reid was made assistant military attaché. A happy event took place when Janey Cabot and Pat Reid married on 28 August 1943. After the war, Pat left the army in the rank of major, and became a successful businessman.

Encouraged by the famous authoress Denise Robins, Pat wrote *The Colditz Story* which was published in July 1952. With the popularity of war stories a film of the same title was produced by Ivan Foxwell and released in 1954 by British Lion. Starring John Mills as Pat Reid, it was a box office success. It boosted the careers of both Mills and Reid who wrote further books on the theme of prisoner-of-war camps and World War Two.

The premier of the film *The Colditz Story* in the presence of Princess Alice served as the first reunion for the veterans of The Colditz Association.

On 19 October 1972 a TV series on Colditz was screened, from an idea by scriptwriter Brian Degas. Gerald Glaister produced it for BBC Television and Universal TV. There were fifteen episodes of fifty minutes starring Edward Hardwicke as Pat Reid, with the box office stars of that time, David McCallum and Robert Wagner, who both appeared from the fourth episode. Pat Reid acted as consultant, the series being based on his two Colditz books.

The first series ended on 25 January 1973 having been an immediate success. A second series was planned and appeared on 7 January 1974 with a further thirteen episodes. Robert Wagner did not at first appear in the series but eventually returned as a major in the US Army. It ended on 1 April 1974. Once again it was a great success and was voted by the *Sun* newspaper readers in their annual award of 1974 as 'the best action series of the year'.

On 14 February 1973 whilst Pat was leaving a meeting at the Europa Hotel, London, he was accosted by an Irishman wearing a trilby pulled over his eyes and a dark bulky overcoat. Pat's companions Degas and Glaister smiled and he was introduced to Eamonn Andrews who revealed that the bulky overcoat in fact contained a red book and Pat was invited to Thames Television for 'This Is Your Life'. Whilst talking to him after the show Pat said his first thought was that he was being kidnapped by the IRA.

Pat Reid teamed up with Brian Degas and a number of spin offs came from the TV series, making Colditz into a highly successful cottage industry. There were endorsements for a board game, video game, Action man, glider, t-shirt and other collectibles. A number of books appeared written by Colditz veterans and others of all nationalities.

Through Pat and the publicity that Colditz received the word became synonymous with 'high security', and the publicity accorded to the camp continues today even after the death of Pat Reid, the man the media called Mr Colditz.

The 'Escape' exhibition at the Imperial War Museum in 2004/05 showing a montage of Colditz collectibles promoted by Pat Reid.

• EIGHT •
DOUGLAS BADER –
MAN OF PURPOSE

It was 9 August 1941 and in the sky over St Omer in France Squadron Leader 'Tin Legs' Bader, wing leader of three squadrons at RAF Tangmere, was engaged, with a squadron of his Spitfires, in mortal combat. Heavily outnumbered by German Me fighters, it was every man for himself. Bader's number two was engaged as Bader dived between six German aircraft. Suddenly he felt a shudder then a resounding bang as his Spitfire spun erratically out of control, the rear portion of his plane broken away. Calmly Bader pushed off his canopy and the air rushed against him; he grasped the sides of his cockpit to roll himself out.

Bader found he was stuck. His right leg was locked beneath his seat. There was no time to undo his uniform and release the brace holding his leg; he had hardly any time before the plane would be too low and he wouldn't be able to bale out. Using all the strength built into his upper body since his horrific crash on 14 December 1931 when he lost his legs, Bader heaved knowing it was his last chance of survival. Superhuman strength built up in his shoulders and there was a crack as the braces snapped on one leg. Wasting no time Bader rolled from the plane; the thought flashed through his mind that he might have damaged his parachute during the struggle. With great relief he found it opened.

As he floated to the ground he had time to ponder on what might have happened. He had seen no German fighter attacking him so the only alternative must have been that one of the German planes he flew past had panicked and in flying an evasive action collided with the rear of his aircraft. The clatter he had heard on being hit hadn't sounded like bullets and the only explanation was another aircraft.

An Me fighter flying towards him interrupted his thoughts. Bader had heard of parachutists being killed in the heat of battle and he thought perhaps now his time had come. Fortunately his luck held and with the chivalry of the air the German pilot turned away.

Bader landed heavily in a field, missing one leg and laid there waiting to be picked up. Soon two Luftwaffe NCOs arrived on a motorcycle with sidecar. Seeing a pilot missing one leg their first reaction was of horror until he pointed out that both his legs were false. They then realised they had captured the British ace Douglas Bader. Notifying St Omer airfield by radio they were ordered by Galland to take him to the main hospital.

In the meantime his rather battered leg, which had fallen out of the wreckage of the plane, was found by a French farmer and handed to the authorities. This was delivered to the hospital where it was fitted as a temporary measure. When he was fit enough Bader was invited by Galland to his airfield for a visit. This was gratefully accepted and the Luftwaffe officers

Bader leaving the airfield after his visit.

Bader is escorted around the airfield base of the German fighter ace Galland, who follows behind with his dog. (*Bader*)

regally entertained Bader to a meal, drinks and a seat in a Me109. All this was photographed for propaganda purposes to appear in *Adler*, the Luftwaffe monthly magazine. The Luftwaffe stated a German pilot officer had shot down Bader. In post-war years a sergeant pilot named Meyer claimed the victory using cannon shells, which could explain the noise and damage. Meyer also stated he flew his Me109 towards the parachutist to see that he was all right. This is what Bader remembered.

In total however, four theories have been suggested in regards to the capture of Bader. The first, stated by Galland, is that Bader was shot down by a Luftwaffe ace. The Luftwaffe officer in question was in fact in combat in another area at the time and recorded a kill there. The second is Bader's own explanation that he had been hit by a German plane whose pilot was taking evasive action. There is no evidence to show this happened. A recent suggestion is that Bader was shot down by 'friendly' fire. I find it hard to believe that an experienced pilot, as the pilot named was, would confuse a British plane with

a German plane. However, such a thing has been known to have happened in the heat of battle. The fourth theory, the claim by Sergeant Pilot Meyer, seems to be the most likely, especially as Bader and Meyer both mention the pilot flying towards the parachutist.

After the visit Bader was returned to St Omer hospital. During this period the Commandant of Dulag Luft (a transit and interrogation camp), Major Rumpel, visited Bader at the hospital. He had been a World War One officer in Goering's squadron, with whom he was friendly. During World War Two Rumpel was one of the senior Luftwaffe intelligence officers. He thought Bader would be a useful member of his permanent staff and asked for contact to be made with England for one of Bader's spare right legs to be flown over to replace the damaged one. Although Rumpel at that time was awaiting court martial for not preventing a mass tunnel escape (the first RAF tunnel escape of the war) from the camp at Whitsun 1941 in which eighteen officers had got free, the German High Command agreed to his suggestion, probably for propaganda purposes. The request illustrates just how badly Rumpel wanted Bader to work for him and in the circumstances was a bold move.

The Commandant of Luftwaffe St Omer was to have a general broadcast transmitted by Station Ushant at 11.35 hrs (GMT) on 13 August 1941. The British Air Ministry therefore received the following message:

"Msg sent by North Foreland Radio 13/8/41.

"Wing Commander Douglas Bader was taken prisoner 9/8/41, lost his right leg whilst baling out. Bader requests that a new leg be sent. Permission granted to drop it by parachute. Time and place of delivery will be fixed from here. Delivering aircraft granted safe conduct."

In the meantime a French girl working at the hospital told Bader that if he ever escaped her parents would give him shelter. Bader duly did so with a rope of bed sheets. True to her word Bader was hidden in a barn.

Unfortunately a fellow worker of the girl betrayed them and Bader was recaptured. The family was ordered to be executed, which was later commuted to life imprisonment in a concentration camp. There is the possibility that this was because Bader was involved. The fact that overtures were still being made for Britain to sue for peace, could have swayed the decision and meant the Germans would not kill people whom Bader would no doubt enquire after when hostilities ended.

However, the publicity Bader had received from the visit to the airfield coupled with his escape gave Himmler the ammunition he was able to use against Goering during a visit to Hitler. Although Galland was one of Hitler and Goering's favourites, he still received a strong reprimand from Goering over the visit.

Air Marshal Dowding spoke to Churchill on the question of parachuting the leg. Both were aware of the standing Bader held with the British public. An Orde drawing of Bader had been used as a front page in the *Illustrated London News* on 19 April 1941. They decided that the leg must be dropped but during a normal raid without safe conduct. So it was that on 19

August during Operation Circus that a Blenheim of 18 Squadron dropped the leg within a crate at 10.30hrs just west of St Omer/Longuenesse aerodrome.

The aircraft had a crew of pilot and captain Sgt Nickelsen, observer Sgt Meadows and air gunner Sgt Pearson. Sgt Pearson performed the actual drop, at some personal risk due to the bulky package. A photograph was taken of the

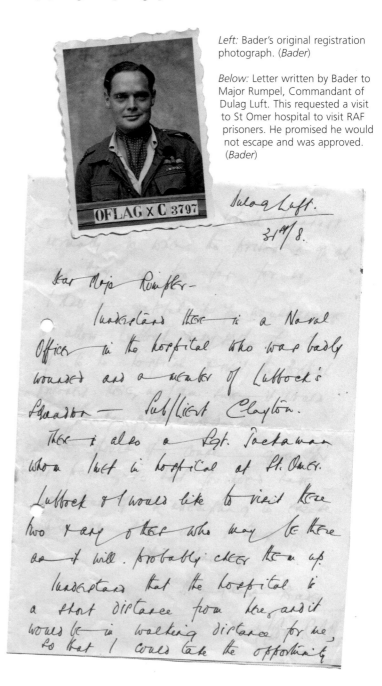

Left: Bader's original registration photograph. (*Bader*)

Below: Letter written by Bader to Major Rumpel, Commandant of Dulag Luft. This requested a visit to St Omer hospital to visit RAF prisoners. He promised he would not escape and was approved. (*Bader*)

Bader's spare leg received in a crate at the request of Major Rumpel. (*Rumpel*)

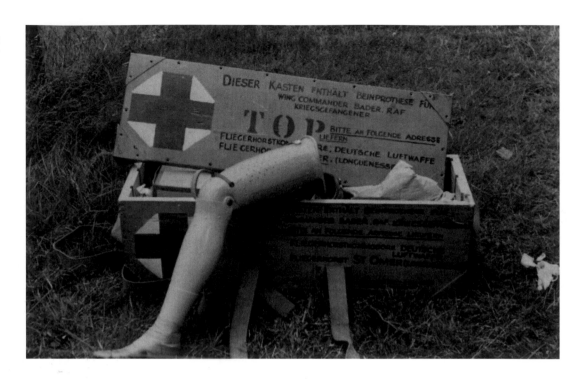

Card written by Bader to Major Rumpel appealing against an impending move from Dulag Luft because of an argument with a Luftwaffe officer at the camp.

Photographs of guard company on parade at Luft III at the time of Bader's move. (*Rumpel*)

crate being parachuted down surrounded by flak. It landed undamaged. Major Rumpel was informed to collect the leg, which he delivered in person to Bader, the day after Bader's arrival at Dulag Luft.

Bader was very direct and demanding in his dealings with the guards. Rumpel would not tolerate this behaviour and after an argument between Bader and a Luftwaffe officer on his staff he ordered his transfer. Realising he had overstepped the mark Bader wrote three notes and asked for an audience with the Commandant to put forward his side. Rumpel ignored them.

Bader was moved to Oflag XC for registration and in October to Oflag IVB at Warburg. When a new secure camp was opened for the RAF at Stalag Luft III Sagan, he was transferred once again in April 1942. There was now no let up in his dealings with the Germans and he expected the other RAF officers to act the same way. When he gave a speech on non-fraternisation with the enemy, the Commandant von Lindeiner had had enough and told Bader he was being transferred to Lamsdorf for medical treatment. Bader refused point blank to budge. Fearing there may be some form of riot the Commandant ordered a full company of guards to be present when Bader was removed.

This resulted in Bader walking out of the compound as though inspecting a guard of honour. It is doubtful if there would have been any reaction as secretly a number of officers were pleased to see the back of him, because of his extensive goon-baiting.

Lamsdorf was at Stalag VIIIB which was a working (Arbeits) camp from where 'Kommandos' were sent to smaller camps. Here Bader teamed up with Flt Lt Johnny Palmer and three others to exchange identities with soldiers due to go to a Kommando at Gleiwitz. Knowing that there was an airfield in that vicinity he intended to steal a plane with Palmer. In August 1942 the identity change was made without a problem and the five escapees arrived at Gleiwitz. The plan was all set when they had a bit of bad luck. A Luftwaffe officer was transferred to an airfield near Lamsdorf; he had met Bader during the visit to St Omer and decided to 'drop in' on his old adversary. He asked permission to visit Bader's hut but on arrival could not find him. The soldier who had switched with Bader was identified as still being at Lamsdorf. Gleiwitz was contacted and all five escapees were unmasked. Bader was placed in a cell next to Mike Moran, a naval officer and persistent escapee. Mike had been one of the main organisers of the Sandbostal tunnel escape. On recapture he was sent to a military prison at Berlin but during the journey escaped. Captured once again he was held in special confinement at Lamsdorf. There he managed to exchange identities with a corporal but was later betrayed. Moran was being held in the cells when Bader arrived.

The decision was made that Bader was too troublesome to hold in an ordinary camp and on 16 August 1942 he arrived at Colditz. Mike Moran followed him on 1 September 1942.

Sqd Ldr Geoffrey Stephenson was an old friend of Bader's; he had been held in Colditz since September 1941. When he saw him arrive he immediately made contact and took him under his wing. The castle and its charges were exactly suited to Douglas's temperament and feelings towards the Germans, because almost everyone was trying to escape and make things difficult for the guards. So he found he was merely an equal among other officers, rather than a one-off nuisance, and settled into prison life.

Bader was able to use his disability to good effect and assisted by Peter Dollar, a major of the 4th Hussars, he would negotiate the cornfields of Colditz on parole with other officers during the harvesting. The only purpose of their presence was to enable Bader to fill his legs with corn for his fellow inmates.

Trumpet practice was also something he tried, the purpose being to assist Pat Reid during his successful escape. The interruptions in practice indicated a guard in the path of the escape route.

Bader still held sway when he thought it necessary and on one occasion instructed the RAF prisoners not to attend talks on communism given by two well known prisoners. It must be admitted that not all the RAF took heed of his instruction, as diversity of lectures was the spice

Card from Mike Moran notifying of his transfer to Colditz.

Kriegsgefangenenlager

Datum: 30. 8. '42

Darling- I shall be moving to an officers' camp tomorrow. The new address will be:-

OFLAG IV C.

GERMANY.

Please let everyone know- including the NEW BODLEIAN LIBRARY· OXFORD ·who send me books.

Tons of love Sweetheart . Tim

Above: RAF group photograph at Colditz. Back row, from left to right: F/Lt Best, F/Lt Forbes, F/Lt Zafouk, F/Lt Flinn, F/Lt van Rood, F/Lt Halifax, F/Lt Donaldson, F/Lt Thom, F/Lt Milne, F/Lt Middleton, F/Lt Goldfinch. Front row, from left to right: F/Lt Dickenson, S/Ldr Stephenson, F/Lt Parker, S/Ldr Bader, S/Ldr McColm, S/Ldr Lockett, F/Lt Bruce. (*Bader*)

Left: Two photographs with a secret camera. *Top,* from left to right: unknown, Campbell-Preston, unknown, unknown, Stayner, Walker, Dollar, Mackenzie, Bader. *Bottom,* from left to right: Walker, Mackenzie, Dollar, Bader, Winn, Gilliat, Pardoe, Hopetoun.

Leaflet received at Colditz to Bader from MI9. This contained the cockpit plans for the Me110. Intercepted by security, Bader's name and the number 1292 are written in blue pencil on the rear of the leaflet, together with a note in German.

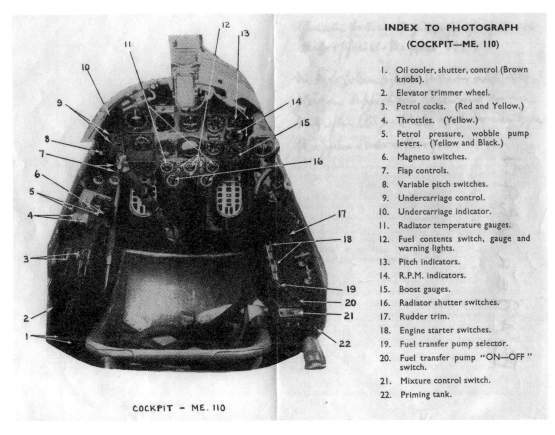

COCKPIT - ME. 110

INDEX TO PHOTOGRAPH
(COCKPIT—ME. 110)

1. Oil cooler, shutter, control (Brown knobs).
2. Elevator trimmer wheel.
3. Petrol cocks. (Red and Yellow.)
4. Throttles. (Yellow.)
5. Petrol pressure, wobble pump levers. (Yellow and Black.)
6. Magneto switches.
7. Flap controls.
8. Variable pitch switches.
9. Undercarriage control.
10. Undercarriage indicator.
11. Radiator temperature gauges.
12. Fuel contents switch, gauge and warning lights.
13. Pitch indicators.
14. R.P.M. indicators.
15. Boost gauges.
16. Radiator shutter switches.
17. Rudder trim.
18. Engine starter switches.
19. Fuel transfer pump selector.
20. Fuel transfer pump "ON—OFF" switch.
21. Mixture control switch.
22. Priming tank.

of life in a closed society. The two prisoners concerned were in fact above reproach in their patriotism, one having received a medal for bravery resulting in his capture. However, Bader expected his particular brand of loyalty from everyone. His loyal and patient orderly Alex Ross bore witness to this, being treated like a skivvy at times and having to fetch and carry for him.

Colditz came under the scrutiny of the War Office and a plan was suggested to arrange for Bader to be out of the castle on a certain date and for a plane to be landed (a Lysander) to pick him up from an autobahn close to the castle. Serious consideration was given to the idea but it was dropped on the suggestion of a Colditz escapee who pointed out the reprisals that might occur for the remaining prisoners if successful, particularly the Prominente. So it was shelved, but the propaganda value of Bader escaping was too big just to be forgotten. It was therefore decided to send Bader the English instructions

for the controls on a Me110. All he had to do was escape from the castle, find an airfield, negotiate the guards, and get to a Me110 unattended, fuelled and ready to fly! Finally, he had to avoid any pursuing aircraft and land safely in allied territory without being blown from the sky. A tall order indeed, and one that failed at its initial stages because the leaflet sent by Clayton-Hutton of MI9 was discovered on its arrival at Colditz. The original was given to me by Eggers and I found written in a German hand and in blue pencil 'Bader 1292' on the reverse. This is an unknown reference number not recognised when shown to Bader.

On the liberation of Colditz, Bader was photographed with a group of RAF fellow prisoners outside the castle. He was then immediately taken to an airfield and flown back to England. Douglas Bader later flew as part of the victory flight for VE day. He was eventually promoted to group captain.

Photograph taken in the prisoners' court-yard, 16 April 1945. Standing, from left to right: Holroyd, Donaldson, Zafouk, Bader, Bufka, Stephenson, Cigos, Parker, Busina. Kneeling, from left to right: Uruba, Truhlar.

Colditz men parade for Bader's memorial service. Amongst those shown are Wilkins, Lockwood, Reid, Anderson, German, Best, Yule, Ferguson, Bruce.

• NINE •
HARRY ELLIOTT – NOTE FROM A DOCTOR

On 18 November 1972 I received a three-page double-sided A4 letter from Harry Elliott. This was written in long hand in answer to some questions I had put to Harry on his escape. It has never been published and is possibly the first time that this unique escape has been told in full. I have copied it as written.

"First, please excuse this awful 'bumph'. I am using it because this is obviously going to be a long screed. You should realise my story can't be made short and it will take a long time.

"Well – I injured my back when captured and though it didn't trouble me much at the time, it started to do so after a year or so. I had cracked vertebrae and arthritis had set in. In our first escape from Oflag VIIC at Laufen, when we 'were out' for nine days sleeping rough etc it wasn't so bad but later I began to realise I couldn't do much 'sleeping rough' and it was very bad weather so I looked around for ways of 'swinging it'.

"About early 1942, someone arrived at Colditz and said the Mixed Medical Commission had been to his camp and the 'grands blesses' had been lined up and some of them had been scheduled for repatriation. So I asked our own POW doctors and they said it must be a disease which one could die of – I mean if one became completely paralysed one need not be in danger of death, as long as one could be kept alive by intravenous feeding etc, and they suggested one or two including 'duodenal ulcer'. I had suffered from that earlier when I was about twenty-five, but had been cured with no recurrence five years before – so that I already knew the symptoms and thought it might not be too difficult.

"The first thing was to go sick pretty often and be seen by the German doctor who came into the camp about four or five times a week. So I attended the sick parade complaining of pains <u>before</u> the next meal and not after it etc etc. After a few weeks of this he told the German medical orderly to have me weighed once a week, every Saturday, and he must see that I wore the same clothes each time. As my idea was to lose weight I had prepared for this by filling my pockets and socks with sand (collected from the fire buckets) with some spares hung around my waist, so I would go and take off various sweaters etc and for the weekly weighing I would wear greatcoat, shirt, trousers, boots and when I went to do this I collected my sand and was back within five minutes to be weighed. Then each week I 'lost' some sand (and weight) but after about six weeks they still were not satisfied, so I had really to lose weight and started starving myself. I was already very thin (I used to weigh about 10st 6lbs and was now down to about 7 stone owing to bad food etc). One POW John Watton was quite a good artist and he made me up to look very ill and after about two weeks I was sent to a POW hospital.

"I didn't know what to expect and when I got there I found most of the POWs were French and Poles but there were a few (about ten) British POWs, all ORs, who told me the POW doctors were Poles and French but there were two Indian doctors. They came to see me directly they heard and I told them I was there as a pretended duodenal ulcer case. So they said they'd help, but were worried about the x-ray – they said the radiologist was French and they didn't trust any of them (French or Poles) who were, they thought, all collaborators. They asked me to have 'tea with them' but regretted they had no tea, but could offer me coffee. Then they said they would take a blood test and stuck a syringe into my vein and drew out a lot of blood and disappeared. They reappeared with the cocoa, which I drank and before leaving they said they had emptied my blood into the cocoa, so I had drunk it, so a test of my 'stool' would show traces of blood.

"Next day my 'stool' was examined and sure enough showed traces of blood i.e. internal bleeding. Then I was sent for an x-ray. The French radio man was very nice and later when I got to know him well, he asked why the hell I hadn't told him, cos he could easily have fixed me up. He told me he was getting lots of cases of duodenal ulcers from the Stalags (OR working camps) and always told each patient to wait until he had developed the x-ray in case it was no good. He could easily put my name on the top of a bad duodenal ulcer photo and do another one for Pierre Dupont or whatever the real owner's name was and no one would ever know.

"The German MO came into the hospital two or three times a week, and when I saw him he said 'no signs of duodenal ulcers in x-ray'. They would keep me a few weeks and give me a diet and about five weeks later I was sent back to Colditz. Then the war went on and on and escaping became harder and harder and all my attempts had failed, so I decided to have another go and this time risk everything and tackle the radiologist, collaborator or not, so the whole process had to start over again, loss of weight etc, etc and eventually I was sent to a POW hospital. This was a different one, exclusively for British and Australian POWs and all the doctors were Australian. I immediately got hold of the radiologist and we walked and walked around a small exercise yard in the snow and I 'sucked up' to him like mad. I told him how my wife had died (quite true), my two little daughters were being looked after by their grandmother and that I simply must get home. Actually their Granny couldn't have done the job better; they loved her dearly and were very happy. I then suggested to him that he should 'fake' my x-ray. He turned on me and said I had no right to ask a thing like that, that he and the other POW doctors and padres were non-combatants and ought to have been repatriated ages ago and there was a rumour that they were to be repatriated in two months' time and that if the Germans got to hear of it, not only would he not be repatriated but he would be sent to a concentration camp and never see Australia again. So I said, 'Sorry – forget about it – sorry – don't think of it again.' Next day I was sent for an x-ray and this Australian did the job and didn't say anything (neither did I). Two days later the German MO appeared and I was sent for and he stuck my x-ray in a sort of frame with a very bright light behind and showed me that I had a 'juicy' duodenal ulcer and he would keep me and I would have to go on a diet for six weeks.

"I kept on friendly terms with the Australian and was eventually told about six weeks later that I must attend next day for another x-ray. So I plucked up my courage and said to this Australian, 'Look old boy, last time my x-ray showed with a nice big ulcer – I do hope that you can repeat this when I come to you tomorrow,' and he said, 'You are a bloody fool, don't you know that duodenal ulcers come and go and after your treatment it would certainly be gone or almost gone – for God's sake shut up.'

"So the next day the deed was done and when I was sent for by the German MO he stuck the x-ray photo in the frame and said, 'There you see, it shows you have responded to treatment, so I will send you back to your camp tomorrow.' But I don't know to this day if the Australian had fixed me up with a fake or not or whether I had actually developed a duodenal ulcer without knowing it. Unfortunately I wrote down the addresses of all POWs I liked and the

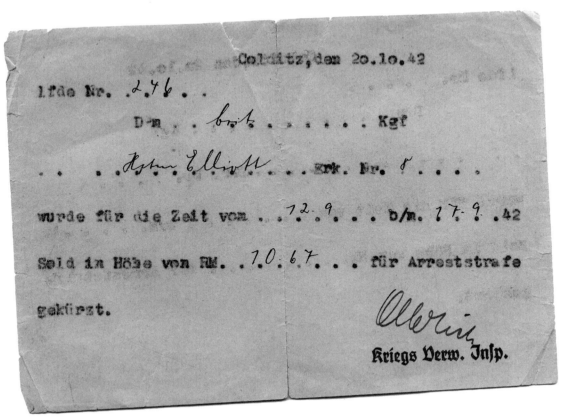

Colditz, den 20.10.42

lfde Nr. 276

D-n . *brit.* . . . . Kgf

. . . . .*Harry Elliott* . . . . Erk. Nr. 8 . . . .

wurde für die Zeit von . .*12.9.* . . b/m. *17.9.* .42

Sold in Höhe von RM. .*10.67*. . . . für Arreststrafe

gekürzt.

Kriegs Verw. Insp.

An order for a deduction of 10RM 67pf for a solitary confinement punishment between 12 and 17 September 1942. Received by Elliott.

Germans took the notebook from me to 'censor it' and I never saw it again – otherwise I would have written to him to thank him and ask him, 'Did you fake my x-ray?'

"Back in Colditz there were about twelve or fifteen cases whom the MO (POWs) wanted to put up to the Mixed Medical Commission if and when it came. It was <u>supposed</u> to go to all camps once a year or the camps were <u>supposed</u> to send their cases to it whenever it was. But the Germans had never allowed our sick to go to it, and so far they had managed to 'put it off' coming to Colditz. However, at last it came about four months after I arrived back there. The night before Silverwood-Cope and I stayed up all night, and I walked up the winding staircase of our quarters, roughly sixty steps once every half hour or so in order to look thoroughly 'shagged out' next day when I appeared before the Commission.

"But the next day there was a row because the Germans refused to let certain POWs present themselves, for instance Douglas Bader (who had no legs – they said it was ridiculous that he could be considered for repatriation) so we said either he was seen by the MMC or none of us would, and we refused to go. The MM Commission was taking place outside in the German part of the camp, and they waited and waited and so did we, none of us went. Finally they sent the German Commandant to ask why and finally he gave in and let all of us appear. My appearance only lasted about a minute and they hardly looked at me (so really all my lack of sleep, Watton's make up etc was unnecessary). They looked at my x-ray and report by the doctors and said I was recommended for repatriation. They did it for about ten POWs and turned down some cases.

"Not long after we were told we would leave next day, only about six of the ten that had been passed were actually allowed to go. Silverwood-

Card sent from Switzerland by Pat Reid to Harry Elliott. Dated 5 November 1944. Pat kept up the pretence of Harry having ulcers by including, "I do think the authorities should see that your ulcers are properly looked after." The postcard shows Pat Reid and his wife photographed with a person in a bear suit (no doubt still referring to bears in a cage). The card was forwarded to the POW hospital for repatriation but Harry had arrived in England before it reached him there, having achieved a home run with a fake repatriation escape.

Cope had been passed but they did not allow him to go, probably because he escaped in Poland and was 'out' for several months and the Gestapo got hold of him and tried to get him to give the names of his contacts. While in their prison, he saw some dreadful atrocities being practised on Poles or on Jews especially and when he got to Colditz he wrote down the whole thing and handed it to the Swiss when they were on their visit as Protecting Power (they came about twice a year). The Germans found out about it and were afraid he would tell people in England etc, etc. Two people who had lost eyes were not passed and several Free French Gaullists who had been badly wounded were passed, but not allowed by the Gestapo.

"I had a red flag against my name – several of us had, and we saw these when we had identification parades and the Germans brought out our POW photographs, which they had taken. The red flags stood for 'Deutsch Feindlich' i.e enemy of Germany. So I am surprised that they allowed me to go.

"We went to the 'Heingangs Lager' where all POWs for repatriation were assembled and finally went by train and crossed to Sweden by ferry and then on a train to Esberg. There we were told we would be put some in hotels, some in barracks and some in boats, until the German POWs arrived from England. Then we were told it would be a man for man exchange so if the number of Germans were less than the number of British some British would have to stay. I was put in a small steamer and we were looked after by some very charming Swedish ladies (Red Cross helpers), given a very good meal and slept in beds with sheets! But I was apprehensive in case the numbers were not equal, because if it came to someone being left behind, it might well be me with my Deutsch Feindlich flag.

"However, next morning we left our respective resting-places and went on the ships, which were to take us back. My ship was about 15,000 tons, Swedish and very comfortable. There were two other ships, one was for bed cases, and another for walking cases, like us. We left about

noon and sailed north up the coast of Norway. The night before we had been able to hear the BBC news which was exciting as the allies had just crossed the Seine and taken Paris. When we asked for the 10 o'clock BBC news the captain said the Germans did not like people hearing the BBC and we were still in German controlled waters. He was afraid of upsetting them and we could not listen in! (I have never felt the same about the Swedes since then.) He did not let us listen until we were 'taken over' and escorted by British destroyers near the Lofoten Islands. The first night out the ship suddenly stopped and a boat came alongside and horrible German voices started shouting orders and hobnailed boots clattered along the passages. I immediately thought of my Deutch Feindlich flag and perhaps they had discovered that the returning Germans were one man short. But luckily that did not happen though we were told that the Germans were looking for a saboteur whom they suspected of stowing away on our ship.

"Eventually we arrived in Liverpool. No parents or friends were allowed to meet us, but on the quay were the Mayor and Corporation mostly in khaki and dozens of women ATS in battledress. We had none of us seen women in battledress before and we were horrified at the way their behinds stuck out in their battledress trousers. All of us were taken to a Military Hospital near Chester and there the walking cases (including me) were given passes to our homes and told we would be notified how much leave we could have. I got a letter from the War Office giving me fourteen days leave! (After more then four and half years as a POW).

"Hitler had refused an exchange of badly wounded in 1940, as he wanted a man for man of badly wounded. Of course after Dunkirk we had more badly wounded then the Germans.

"The wretched men were returned to Germany. There were only two repatriations during the war to my knowledge, 1942 and the last one that I got back on in October 1944. Incidentally my Mixed Commission consisted of two Swiss and two German doctors."

TEN

HAIR FOR A LADY

During the sixties I received an invitation to the Sikorski museum in London from a Polish veteran of Colditz Castle POW camp. He introduced me to an official who had also been held at Colditz. Prior to leaving he took from his drawer two items which he gave to me. The first was a china mug that he had used as a prisoner; the second was an unpublished manuscript. It gave background information to a unique French escape attempt and was written by an unknown author. This is that story.

"The beautifully illustrated book *Castles in Saxony* describes the fortress at Colditz, stressing the architectural merits and praising its imposing site but then goes on to state that the castle is lacking in amenities. This will not surprise anyone acquainted with its recent history for it had been used in turn as a lunatic asylum, a place of detention for German Communists, then for Czech officers, later still for Polish ones and eventually the 'Sonderlager', or special camp for French, British, Belgium, Polish, Dutch and Yugoslav officers alike. It was known as Oflag IVC and in it was a great many prisoners who because of some outstanding feat the Germans wished to keep in an especially safe place. Most had one or two escapes, or attempted escapes to their credit, but there were also some whose crime was 'political agitation', the 'inciting of fellow prisoners' or 'hostility to the German Reich'.

"Thus there was collected in one place a group of men with more than average brains and initiative and a great deal of escaping experience. So that in time the camp became a veritable school in the art of escaping with all the requisite workshops from which by devious ways the hard-acquired knowledge was diffused to other camps in Germany. In the camp itself the fever of continual escape preparations was so contagious that even men not usually enterprising were seized by it and made their own plans for getting out of the well-guarded castle.

"The extreme overcrowding in the castle which housed well over 600 prisoners was one more reason for getting out of it. The prisoners spent most of their time in the cobbled courtyard shut in on all sides by the high castle walls. Only once a day, for an hour and a half, they were allowed to go to the park near the castle, but the lengthy checking and rechecking by the guards, both before and after the outing as well as their presence with arms at the ready, detracted from the pleasure and many preferred to stay in the courtyard. There, on sunny days, they spread themselves out on the ground and talked interminably of the war, or reminisced at length.

"On one such sunny day late in the summer of 1941, when I was looking for an empty space on the cobblestones, I heard myself addressed in French. I looked up and saw a rather corpulent person wearing dark glasses inviting me to a place under the wall next to him. I thanked him and sat down and introduced myself. He did likewise and I heard a French name, which sounded suspiciously like 'Bunny Bun' [his name was Lieutenant Boulay]. I shook his hand and for the next few minutes gave myself up to the silent enjoyment of the warm sunshine.

"My companion would not have been French however had he not struck up a conversation, in the course of which he told me his past story and how he got to Colditz.

"Having been taken prisoner by the Germans he was sent to a camp in Poland, near Poznan, where he established contact with Polish workers who came to the camp to work, and with their encouragement and help he and his friends began to collect an escape kit. All went well and a quantity of civilian clothes was all ready in the camp when the Germans found them in their possession and as a reprisal sent him and his friend to Colditz.

"It was his first week there. I had listened carefully to his story and when he had finished I ventured to criticise the way in which they had covered up their preparations and I was just about to say that much better ways could have been found when I was interrupted by the sad shaking of his head. 'No,' he said, 'On n'avait pas de chance,' and he repeated this several times, adding that without luck the best laid plans would come to nought.

"As if to illustrate this theory he related his own case history. Just as he was beginning to see light in his business ventures in France, the war broke out and set him back where he had started. Here with a flourish he explained that he was not one of those who did not want to die for Danzig. No, for him the war was a serious business and the fight against the Boches had to be carried to the end, but did anyone foresee that for France that end would be so tragic and swift? There again luck was not with him. With his companion he had been at Dunkirk to cover the withdrawal of the British and while the latter made a splendid job of it, he, and his company with him, found themselves prisoners of the Germans. And what was to blame if not his unlucky star? So many of his friends had quietly gone home having conveniently doffed their uniforms, but with his luck he had to become a POW. At this point his story was punctuated by

a loud 'bad luck' occasioned by some incident in a game of volleyball, and Bunny Bun sadly shook his head as if taking that random cry for confirmation of his melancholy story.

"After a short pause, he raised himself on his elbow, turned towards me and peering from behind his dark glasses unexpectedly confided, 'You see, I am quite unfitted for a prisoner's life.'

"'And who is?' I put in a matter of fact tone before he continued his sad tale.

"'Quite right, quite right,' he said, 'no one probably is, for every one treasures freedom above everything else. But in my case,' and his voice trailed off. Then taking up the thread of his narrative with renewed vigour he continued.

"'I have a wife and young children, am a business man employing many people, with custom it has taken me many years to build up, and no one to take care of anything.' He paused and then said: 'The work of a lifetime going to

Lieutenant Boulay photographed by the Germans in his fake disguise.

ruin…. The Jerries running everything and robbing everybody, and I, here helpless.' Again his voice broke and he was silent for a time. But as if unable to stop the flow of his recriminations he spoke again, 'I don't even write to my wife, as the knowledge that someone will read what I write prevents me from doing it. I have to stay here, bear the company of people I don't know and don't wish to know and feed on that German filth. Have you heard of humans eating turnips? I ask you! Or badly boiled carrots. I have had more than enough of it and this war looks like going on for years. Just my rotten luck.' He sighed deeply and fell back limply on his blanket.

"I had not interrupted this outburst of bitterness, as he was not the only one to take this imprisonment in this hard way. He was perhaps amusing in his grudges against fate but on the whole he was sympathetic, human and so authentically French. When sometime later he took up his blanket to go in, his eyes fell on the sandals I wore on my feet.

"'Those come from Poland?' he asked.

"'Yes, I took them instead of my slippers and they are proving very useful,' I answered.

"'They are very well made,' he remarked, still looking at them. 'They are from Warsaw I dare say,' he continued.

"'No,' I said, 'I got them in a small provincial town.' But I concurred that they were a neat job.

"'Yes, very neat,' said my Frenchman, 'and they would probably fit me as well. I have very small feet for my height,' he explained.

"I looked at his feet encased in military boots caked in what probably was still the Dunkirk mud and agreed with his judgement as to their size.

"The Frenchman stood there for a while longer then he bid me goodbye distractedly and sauntered off.

"A few days later one of my friends standing at a window suddenly exclaimed, 'I say, look here, Paddy's gone hopping mad!' 'Who?' someone asked.

"'Paddy, Paddy Chancey,' he explained, as such was the nickname we had given to the unfortunate Frenchman who began and ended all his conversations with the despondent 'pas de chance'. And what was more remarkable, the nickname had been given by some of my friends who spoke no French but who nevertheless had been intrigued by this oft repeated phrase to have so adapted it for their convenience. I looked out of the window and in the now deserted yard I saw Bunny Bun. He was pacing up and down, taking short little steps, keeping his knees together and his elbows well in, while at the same time his head swayed gently on his rather short neck in a swan-like fashion as he walked looking neither right nor left, his eyes on the ground in front of him, apparently oblivious of everything around him.

"From that time on I started keeping a discreet watch over my French aquaintance. He kept up his habit of lonely walks in the courtyard but otherwise he seemed to become completely engrossed in work in the wardrobe of the camp theatre. He became known as a keen helper of a French captain, formerly dress designer to a famous Paris theatre and creator of many masterpieces of frilly tissue paper and of wigs of unwoven strings. We still met in the park quite often and when we did, talked of our worries and hopes.

"One day before the morning roll call, a friend came up to me looking very mysterious and said that a French prisoner had seen my sandals and would be very obliged if I let him have them 'for the known purpose'. Unfortunately at that time I no longer possessed them and I explained to my friend that I was very sorry not to be able to help. As we came down to roll call we noticed an unusual commotion among the Frenchmen. One young officer was being mobbed by the rest of them and as we drew near we recognised him as a young Jewish student of philosophy who fulfilled the function of rabbi among his correligionists and who had grown a long silky beard as a sign of sorrow after being taken captive. Now he appeared without it and was the centre of a joyous group, greeting him with prolonged howling, cat calls and questions whether he was not cold and whether his inner balance was not shaken by the loss of so imposing an ornament. In the monotony of camp life even the least thing gave way to mirth and this proved no exception.

"The summer was warm and sunny and walks in the park were becoming increasingly popular, but in spite of that one day a discreet request to turn out in force for the daily outing was passed from group to group. Of course everybody knew what that meant. The Germans were to be prevented from making an accurate count of those going to the park so that one could stay behind and make his escape. The covering up of the roll call later was done in a different way and the escapee had some time in hand before his absence was discovered and the chase given.

"Accordingly, so great a crowd assembled for the outing that the German officer in charge showed surprise and it had to be explained to him that the heat in the castle was unbearable, and that the British had an important football match to play that afternoon. Officers dressed in shorts and jerseys kept joining the column all the time and the counting had to be repeated several times. At last the German officer, who had become irritable, had everybody file out through the courtyard gate and began the counting once more outside the guardroom windows. There the players and their public formed into the regulation five ranks, but still more variously dressed men emerged through the gate and fell in with the rest.

"Truly, the most patient of men would have despaired that afternoon. Because of the great heat the standard of dress varied widely, though almost everybody wore sunglasses and many carried blankets and military pillows, conspicuous by their large check covers. One enormous Dutchman with a grey patriarchal beard towered above the heads of his companions, swathed in a long cape reaching almost to the ground. Only a small number knew that under the cape and the beard a young and small Polish lieutenant, little Eddie, stood on the giant's feet and would take the place of the man who was to escape at the return count.

"I stood in the fourth row, and as I waited for the column to set out I looked around trying to guess who it was that wished to leave us that day. As I looked I saw a pair of small reddish shoes not far on my right, and in them two rather muscular but quite shapely legs covered by light silk stockings. As I looked up my eyes fell on that part of a personal wardrobe that used not to be mentioned in Victorian days, neatly fashioned out of the corresponding masculine garment, and higher still began a very voluminous blouse of a military appearance, though devoid of any markings denoting either rank or nationality. Out of the collar protruded a head, but only just, and it too was almost hidden by an enormous Polish four-cornered cap and a pair of large sunglasses.

"I recognised Bunny Bun and guessed that the word must have been passed round for his sake. He stood quite motionless as if lost in deep meditation. Under the visor of his cap his pink, carefully shaved cheek twitched slightly and in front of him he held a thick blanket folded over several times. His neighbours, (he stood in the third row, right in the centre of the column), were all very noisy and fidgety and whenever the German NCO counting us passed them they did their best to cover up their friend in the middle.

"At last the final count was taken, the German officer on duty received the NCOs' report, little Eddie ducked neatly out from under the Dutchman's cape and the column moved towards the park. To get there it had to pass through the outer courtyard of the castle from which one gateway led straight into the village of Colditz whose houses began directly outside it. The entrance to the camp Commandant's office was situated just before that gate and in front of it a sentry always stood on guard by his striped sentry box. Further to the left another gateway led to the castle gardens and to the park. It was long and dark and cluttered up with old carts and various agricultural implements. Beside the road to the park, on the other side of the castle walls were the NCOs' married quarters and we often met German women and children while going for our daily outing.

"Whenever such a meeting took place the German NCO accompanying us used to ask the woman to pass quickly as a meeting of that kind might perhaps be too much for officers, some of them with over two years in captivity. (After all, each and every one of us had signed a solemn undertaking not to have any truck with German womenfolk under the pain of death.) In the course of transit from the castle to the park our escort walked on the left side only so as not to wound any of their own men should any shooting follow an escape attempt.

"We had passed the courtyard outside the Commandant's office and the column entered the dark gateway beyond. When Paddy Chancey was in its darkest place loud laughter and jeers

The female disguise of Boulay on display in the camp museum. Note that there are other items from the collection on the desk.

were heard at both ends of the column which distracted the attention of the guards. Then someone quickly took Paddy's blanket, someone else snatched off his voluminous blouse, revealing underneath a smart grey jacket with black trimmings: with a tug a neighbour pulled down the matching skirt which till then had been rolled up, while under the jacket I noticed a very coquettish frilly white blouse. From under the blanket the theatrical dress designer pulled a wide brimmed black hat with hair attached and with one skilful movement placed it on Paddy's head. A black shiny handbag thrust into his hands and a pair of black gloves completed a very convincing whole.

"The shapely fraulein was pushed out of the marching ranks and as the remarks made by the Frenchmen at her sight became louder the German NCO noticed her presence and coming up asked her courteously to pass through to the courtyard leading to the town. Looking very embarrassed and shy, his eyes on the ground, Paddy walked along as requested, taking short mincing steps towards the gateway to freedom.

"Even those who had helped the metamorphosis were hard put to it to realise how successfully the whole thing came off. Everything was over so quickly that there was no time to look back to see what would happen. Anyway, once beyond the gateway the road to the park turned sharply and with the thick castle walls in between nothing more could be seen.

"Once in the park we were recounted, but as little Eddie had by now taken Paddy Chancey's place the numbers agreed and we broke ranks and scattered to our various pursuits. The game of football and various forms of PT soon claimed those of an energetic disposition while others walked under the trees or sprawled on the grass. Only those in the know were tense and could find nothing to distract them from their anxiety for the success of the escape.

"Having emerged from under the dark archway the plump German miss proceeded straight towards the outer gate. She had to pass in front of the sentry box and the houses on the other side were already in sight, when a German NCO emerged from the guard room escorting a few latecomers to the park. As they passed the young woman crossing the yard, one of them, an RAF officer, saw that she had dropped her wristwatch and in his broken German tried to attract her attention to the fact. As she pressed on however without seeming to hear, the German NCO picked up the watch and in a loud voice spoke to her again. But Paddy, who hardly spoke German, lost his head and forged ahead regardless. At this stage the sentry at the box joined in and when a moment later all three of them appeared in front of him, Paddy's embarrassment was so obvious that he was asked about his pass and eventually he was taken to the camp offices where his identity was discovered.

"The RAF officer who spotted the watch, himself a veteran of several unsuccessful escapes, was disconsolate and for days after his mouth was twisted into a perpetual 'sorry'.

"The camp security officer, endowed with a sense of humour unusual in a German, first of all congratulated Paddy on his appearance, then paid compliments to his readiness to brave the many complications that his assumed role would have exposed him to, and lastly expressed his regrets that so ingenious and so carefully prepared a plan had ended in failure.

"To which I am sure he must have heard a subdued but now poignant, 'Pas de chance, helas, pas de chance.'

"Photographs were taken showing Paddy in the full bloom of his feminine attire, both with and without his hat, the latter shot not altogether without malice for he was well on the way to complete baldness. At his insistence however the camp authorities agreed not to sell the photographs to the prisoners, who could buy those illustrating the castle, without his permission.

"The photographs together with the costume draped on a dummy became the prized exhibits of the camp escape museum established to train the personnel and drew gasps of astonishment from the civilians admitted to it on visiting days, as well as smiles of pride that the cleverness of the guards had prevailed over the prisoner's cunning.

"When we returned from the park, Paddy Chancey looking very downcast stood by the guardroom door already dressed in his uniform, waiting to be escorted to the solitary detention cells. In accordance with the rules he had a fortnight's solitary confinement awaiting him as punishment for a second escape attempt. As the British RAF officer had naturally told his story in the park everybody knew of Paddy's discomfort and had something to say to cheer him up, but he only shook his head sadly and repeated, 'It 'as to be expected, just my hard luck. Pas de chance.'

"The investigation carried out by the Germans revealed that the feminine attire had belonged to the wardrobe of a theatre probably dating back to the days of the lunatic asylum, of which the camp authorities had been completely unaware. As for the hair, which had so becomingly transformed the middle-aged Frenchman, it had come from the long and flowing beard of the Jewish philosopher who willingly sacrificed it when asked to help a friend's escape. Photographs of the latter, both with and without beard, with the explanation to what a vile use it had been put were appended to the case records in the escape museum.

"After the period of his solitary confinement was over, Bunny Bun was taking the air at my side in the castle courtyard one day when suddenly he stopped and gripping my arm said, 'If only I had had your sandals for my escape I am sure it would have succeeded. It was when I saw them on your feet that the idea of the disguise occurred to me.'

"Sometime later we learned that thanks to the intercession of the Vichy government all French prisoners with large families were to be released, and as Bunny Bun had three sons he was to be included in their number. As soon as I learned of this I rushed to him and found him already packing his belongings. Early the next morning he was to leave for the transit camp. I of course congratulated him on such a fortunate turn of events only to be met with an expression of unutterable sadness on his face.

"'You must be making fun at my expense, my friend,' he said reproachfully. 'I wished of course to return to France, but not with the German's consent and under their supervision. Why, this will very likely stamp me as a collaborator and I shan't even be able to look my kids straight in the eye. Again my rotten luck!'

"He thought for a moment and then said, 'I suppose I shall have to make a dash for North Africa at the first opportunity, that is, if with my luck the Germans don't get me on the way.'

"And on this rather pessimistic note we parted forever, for I never saw him again.

• ELEVEN •
MIKE SINCLAIR –
THE GREAT ESCAPER

Lieutenant Albert Michael Sinclair, known as 'Mike' to his friends, was born in 1918. The second of three sons, his father was a soldier and his mother came from a distinguished military family. With the rise of Hitler's Germany the three boys joined the Army as soon as they were of age. All three served with distinction, with the youngest, John, giving his life at Anzio in 1944. The eldest son Christopher, although captured by Rommel's forces, managed to escape with two wounded prisoners, being awarded an MC, to which a bar was added later in the war. He retired a lieutenant colonel.

Mike Sinclair was a scout platoon commander in France in 1940. It was at Calais, when he was commander of A Platoon with his friend Lt Gris Davies-Scourfield, commander of B Platoon, that they came under a sustained attack by Panzers. The regiment of the 60th Rifles gave a good account of themselves fighting a rearguard action for the evacuation at Dunkirk. They held back what was expected to be a sweeping German advance for two days. Eventually they were overwhelmed and Mike and Gris became prisoners of war.

Taken to Laufen POW camp they found fellow 60th officer Ronnie Littledale, and were both invited by Littledale to join him in a tunnel escape. This they did but were caught before the tunnel was complete. Sentenced to solitary they were taken out before completion of sentence and with other officers, including Littledale who had not been discovered in the tunnel attempt, were sent to a reprisal camp at Posen, known as Fort 8. Here the prisoners were kept in chains for periods of time for alleged ill treatment of German POWs at Fort Henry in Canada. After a visit by the German POW escapee von Werra,

who stated this had not been the case, the treatment stopped.

A further opportunity to escape then became available for Sinclair, Littledale and Davies-Scourfield – in a rubbish cart – and was to be attempted separately. Mike left on 28 May 1941.

Having obtained a contact name whilst in Posen the three escapees were destined to spend several months with the Polish underground. They were constantly moved from safe house to safe house whilst waiting for an opportunity to leave for England.

Mrs Elizabeth Odorkiewicz of Katowice wrote of the Posen three: "We did not know where they came from or where they went. There was a conspiracy, even in family life, not to mention names and addresses even in conversation with each other. My husband wrote a book in 1945 on his activities with escapes of British and American POWs. Mr Winton [Peter Winton, another Colditz man], one of our 'guests', after the war gave us some information for the book which he had got from the Gestapo at Lodz."

Mrs Luciyna Lutostanska of Warsaw wrote: "My husband did not know where they went. His

Mike Sinclair in Colditz.

sister Zula brought them to us and took them away. She died in 1943."

There was great danger in harbouring an escapee. With continuous movement over several months the strain on Mike would have been almost intolerable too.

Mike and Ronnie were in Budapest when they were separated from Gris, and were taken to Bulgaria. On 27 November 1941, after a number of adventures, Bulgarian police arrested them. Although they were promised contact with the American embassy they were in fact handed over to the Germans. Taken to Vienna they were then transported to Dresden. During the train journey they seized an opportunity and both jumped from the train. Mike was soon recaptured whilst Ronnie escaped.

Handed over to the Gestapo, Mike was kept in custody and questioned until January 1942. Then after interrogation he was taken under escort to Colditz. He was joined by Davies-Scourfield in March who had also suffered a similar fate. Captured in Cracow he had been taken by the SS for lengthy interrogation after which he was placed in a prison with no hope of release. Fortunately he made himself known to a visiting German general and was later taken under escort to Colditz. Littledale arrived in July, although they could only keep him three months before he made a home run as part of the Pat Reid team. He was later killed commanding a battalion in France in 1944.

Mike Sinclair was completely unselfish in his escape activities and his dedication to escape was planned to the last detail.

Gris Davies-Scourfield wrote: "He had a very strong character and once he had set his mind to something would never give up. The main driving force behind his efforts was undoubtedly a sense of duty. There was no disgrace whatsoever to his capture. Nevertheless, he himself felt the humiliation bitterly and firmly believed that he could only make up for his humiliation by escaping successfully and fighting again. Although he was extremely intelligent and indeed highly intellectual, possessing a brilliant scholastic mind and great ability for languages, he did absolutely nothing during his prison existence except to plan and attempt to escape."

If anyone wanted advice to escape then Mike would give them every assistance. He normally made his escapes with companions, on one occasion being the architect of one which became known as the Franz Joseph affair.

This escape involved the impersonation of the guard Sergeant Rothenberger, who with his auburn hair and bushy moustache was nicknamed 'Franz Joseph' by both prisoners and guards alike, after the Emperor of Austria. Mike's hair colour was similar. He had to imitate the German sergeant's 'strut', mannerisms and voice. He gave himself over completely to this task until he was satisfied he could pass as the man. In the meantime the German uniforms had to be made or 'obtained', for Sinclair and his two 'guards' Hyde-Thompson and Pope. They had to be perfect and were hidden in the radio hide. An RAF cap was sacrificed to make Rothenberger's headgear, green paint was used and the cap badge cut from thin wood and painted also.

Major Anderson wrote: "Scarlet O'Hara and I were responsible for making two rifles and pistols, together with the bayonet scabbards. Scarlet would stand behind a guard during their searches of our barracks with a piece of string and measure the length of various parts of the rifle. The rifles were made from bed boards. The 'steel' parts were carved out of tin from the Red Cross parcels and the bolt and stock were made separately. I remember that a fairly good metallic finish was achieved by rubbing in soft pencil lead and polishing – the dark wood stain would undoubtfully have been achieved with Pot Pormay from the Revier [the hospital], followed by German bootpolish. The sling would have been of real leather. All work went on in one room in the British quarters very carefully stooged, with a good hide very handy in case of spot searches. Belts and revolver holsters were Scarlet O'Hara's specialities, and he took an enormous pride in them – 'This one is a real honey,' I remember him saying as he fondled it lovingly! I think he rather hated parting with them. Carving the excellent quality lino from the German floors was my particular line, for Ausweis stamps and cap badges."

On the evening of 2 September 1943 the

Items used in the Franz Joseph escape. An RAF cap was altered to represent Rothenberger's cap. The rifle was made from bed boards by Major Anderson. The scabbard and bayonet used by Sinclair are shown, as is a brush with green paint which was used for the cap, and Mike's regimental tobacco pouch.

plan was put into action. Having gained entry to the eastern terrace from a window where the bars had been cut from razor blade hacksaws, the two 'sentries' Hyde-Thompson and Lance Pope followed the 'sergeant' Mike Sinclair, to relieve the sentries at the park gate and catwalk above. Walking to the guard at the gate he told him to hand over his keys and return with the catwalk guard to the Kommandantur to answer questions about an earlier escape. Mike was handed the keys but the guard seemed suspicious and asked for his pass. This was the weakness in the plan. They had copied a genuine pass but knew the colour of the card was changed occasionally. They also knew that all sentries had to ask for a pass from an officer they did not know. To be on the safe side they chose guards that they knew to be part of Rothenberger's platoon and therefore would not ask for the pass. It was a gamble that didn't pay off. Mike with a lot of shouting knew he had no alternative and drew the sentry to a dark area and produced the pass. The sentry however took it into the light and then asked Mike for the 'Parole' (watchword) of the day. An argument took place and then the guard shouted to the catwalk guard to sound the alarm.

Peter Hofmann wrote: "I was on duty when the alarm rang. Sentries 5 and 6 were at the park gate. They saluted Sinclair and then were told to hand over the keys; they were relieved. We had recently been instructed because of the number of impersonations always to ask for the 'Parole' of the day, from everyone no matter who they were. Sinclair did not know it. An argument broke out and sentry 6A on the wooden bridge rang the alarm. Unteroffizier Pilz arrived and during the exchange of words Sinclair apparently went for his holster and was shot." Sinclair was wounded in the chest. Pilz later died on the Russian front.

What raised the guard's suspicion? It is suggested Rothenberger had a habit, when he reached this particular post, of pausing before approaching and looking out across the forest, which only the guard would recognise. It obviously was not done, did this raise a doubt in his mind? Although he had examined the pass in the dark, which had been deliberate on Mike's part, the guard then took it away to examine under the light. The pass was grey when it should have been yellow. It was then he was challenged for the 'Parole' word, which Mike obviously didn't know. In addition Pilz knew that a number was added serially at the bottom of the card in tiny figures. It was thought to be a printer's number by the forgers but in fact was different for each pass. The final straw was that both the guard and Pilz knew that Rothenberger's Christian name was Gustav not Fritz as shown on the card.

It is reported that one rifle was smashed, possibly over the head of Hyde-Thompson, whilst the other survived. Mike Sinclair wrote in his evidence of the shooting at the time:

"I was shot whilst my hands were up. I was then thrown into a solitary confinement cell and only after protests to two German officers was an ambulance called to take me to hospital. I was x-rayed and then returned to the camp. Whilst being placed in the ambulance I was kicked in the head."

Once Mike had recovered he soon returned to his escaping activities. With his red hair and his reputation the Germans knew him as the 'Red Fox'. His photograph was circulated to all security points within a radius of Colditz. Mike concentrated more and more on escaping, and it was noticed how his pipe stems were being chewed and his regimental pouch was being used regularly to fill the pipe as he smoked and thought hard. But he still kept to his careful planning.

An example is described by Gris Davies-Scourfield: "When Mike Sinclair and Jack Best escaped in 1943 down the side of the castle on ropes, there were 70 stooges (look-outs) on duty at various points all over the castle to make certain that the escapees could not be seen. This escape had to be called off at the last moment on several occasions because one or more of the stooges reported conditions in his sector unfavourable. The escape was carried out successfully, though both escapees were subsequently recaptured at the Rhine and returned to Colditz."

Finally Mike's most daring escape from within Colditz park was attempted alone. He knew of the high risk and would not endanger a companion.

Gris Davies-Scourfield wrote, "His final and fatal escape was not known by anyone — even me. It was a very risky one and if he had told anyone about it they would have tried to dissuade him. But it was a calculated risk — he always calculated everything minutely. I was in the castle when I heard firing. There was quite a lot of it as Mike ran the gauntlet. He was unlucky to be hit and even unluckier not to have been merely wounded."

Kenneth Lockwood, responsible for escape money, said that as he walked in the prisoners' yard before the park walk, Mike stopped him and asked for some German money. Kenneth had not been told an escape was in the offing but knowing Mike, he immediately went to his cache and returned with the required amount.

Mike is reported to have been wearing a long cloak and when he was in the prisoners' enclosure within the park he detached himself from the others. Mike Moran states he was standing on the rise within the enclosure and on seeing Mike standing alone approached him. "He turned and quite abruptly said 'Can't you go somewhere else?' Looking at Mike I realised something was happening and replied 'Sorry Mike' before

The concrete post climbed by Sinclair in his fatal attempt, photographed in 1980. It has since been removed by the authorities.

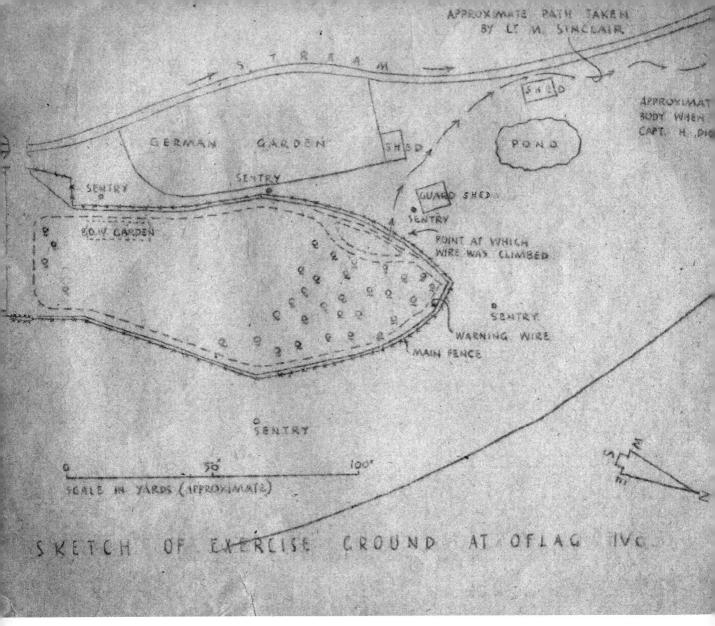

APPROXIMATE PATH TAKEN
BY LT M. SINCLAIR

S T R E A M

GERMAN GARDEN

SHED

SHED

POND

APPROXIMAT
BODY WHEN
CAPT. H. DI

SENTRY

SENTRY

BOW GARDEN

GUARD SHED

SENTRY

POINT AT WHICH
WIRE WAS CLIMBED

SENTRY

WARNING WIRE

MAIN FENCE

SENTRY

0   50'   100'

SCALE IN YARDS (APPROXIMATE)

SKETCH OF EXERCISE GROUND AT OFLAG IVC

Original sketch plan made after the death of Mike Sinclair, showing his escape attempt.

returning to the rise, taking out my pipe and lighting up. Turning around I saw him; he was wearing gloves, he put one hand on the concrete post, the other on the wire where the bolt was attached to the post, and pulled himself up and over. It took seconds then crouching down he ran zig-zagging past the hut towards the boundary wall where the stream runs under the road. He was spotted and the firing began. He almost made it but then he stumbled and fell, he had been hit. Later we were told that a bullet had struck the elbow bone and deflected into his heart. He died instantly. I was the last person to speak to him."

Captain Dickie of the RAMC was called and confirmed that Sinclair was dead. It was 25 September 1943. Albert Michael Sinclair was twenty-six. The 'Red Fox' was free.

Three days later the order for the Burial of the Dead was held in the town church and cemetery. All the members of the 60th Regiment were allowed to attend the service. A lesson from *Pilgrim's Progress* chosen by Davies-Scourfield was read. Sinclair was buried with full military honours. His body was laid to rest after the war at the British Military Cemetery in Berlin.

For his parents to have two sons killed in the same year was a terrible tragedy. His elder brother wrote sadly, "I went abroad in December 1938 and did not see my brother from that time on."

John Watton, the Colditz artist, sent a portrait he made of Mike to Christopher Sinclair in 1942.

With the end of World War Two the task was set to trace and acknowledge all those that had served above and beyond the call of duty. Many were to be honoured posthumously.

Major General Victor Fortune, the most senior British officer, and a prisoner of the Germans in World War Two, on writing his recommendation for a posthumous bravery award to Lt Albert Michael Sinclair, wrote that in his opinion the officer was the greatest British Army escapee in the war. Four senior officers, including Brigadier Davies of Colditz and Lt Colonel Tod the Senior British Officer also endorsed this. Also included were two other Senior British Officers of POW camps. A unique posthumous DSO was awarded.

Mike Sinclair's award was richly deserved. In my opinion there are two other armed services representatives eligible for this honour, Jimmy Buckley of the Royal Navy and Roger Bushell of the Royal Air Force. They all had one thing in common, complete dedication to escaping and all three paid the ultimate sacrifice as the greatest escapees of World War Two.

Portrait of Sinclair drawn by John Watton.

The grave of Lieutenant A.M. Sinclair at the British Military Cemetery, Berlin.

• TWELVE •
A COCKNEY IN COLDITZ

I first made contact with Sidney Goldman in the late sixties. Knowing of the reputation he had earned in Colditz, I was thrilled to have traced him through his younger brother Alf to a town in America. We immediately hit it off and corresponded regularly. It was at the beginning of 1970 that he wrote informing me in confidence that he had been diagnosed as having stomach cancer and been given about six months. His ambition was to visit London one last time and meet up with some of the officers he had lived with in Colditz. On 10 July 1970 'Solly', as his friends knew him, landed at Heathrow. Arrangements had been made for a luncheon meeting at the Army and Navy Club with his Colditz friends. I accompanied Solly and was able to meet for the first time as a group such people as Guy German, Rupert Barry, Pat Reid, Airey Neave, Dick Howe, and about half a dozen more.

Later at my home Solly and I settled down and he told me the story of his war. This was first produced in a police magazine called *The Warren* in 1971, when I was still a policeman. Here is an abridged version.

Sidney twisted in the slip trench to lie on his back. Grasping the butt of his rifle between his knees, he lovingly wiped the mud from the barrel. The gunfire had died away to be replaced by the soft patter of rain upon the mud. It was May 1940 and the Royal Fusiliers were on a rear defence action at Arras in France.

'Bleeding weather,' he muttered. 'Hey sarge,' he called out, 'what's the date?'

'Twenty-sixth,' came the gruff reply followed by, 'Why do you want to know, you're not going anywhere.'

'Blimey,' thought Sidney. 'This time last year I was down the Lane with me barrow and this bleeding war was just a load of hot air. Now I'm stuck in this stinking hole in France.'

The sound of automatic weapons started again, much closer this time.

'Hey, sarge, if a kraut walks over this trench do you think he would mind if I shoved me rifle up him and shot some sense into him?'

Sergeant Clayton smiled and spat into the puddle at his feet. He glanced across at the youngster and thought to himself, 'Have a joke Solly my lad, with the krauts all over us if a bullet hasn't got your name on it then Hitler's butchers will make short work of your Jewish carcass.'

Sidney continued to wipe his rifle until he heard a sharp crack. Smoke curled from Clayton's rifle as a German buckled at the knees and tumbled into the trench. Two more Germans appeared at the other side of Clayton. A third loomed over Sidney and he threw up his rifle, firing at the intruder. The German twisted, screaming in agony, Sidney fired again, silencing him. He just had time to see Clayton squirming in the mud, blood pumping from a wound in his

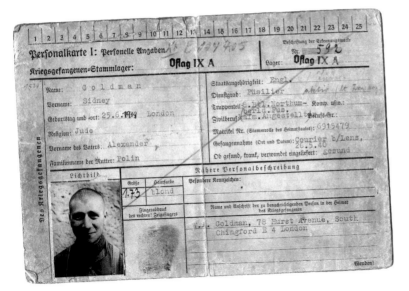

Sidney 'Solly' Goldman's POW identification card. Note under religion it states Jude.

neck. A quick shot from the hip caught a German in the arm, as he was about to fire at him. Suddenly he felt a sharp searing pain enter his bowels which became more intense as the German withdrew his bayonet. The rifle dropped from Sidney's hands as he tried desperately to stem the flow of blood. Rolling over his helmet fell from his head, his blond hair falling across his eyes. The German raised his rifle to stab again.

Sidney opened his eyes to see a nurse and what he assumed was a doctor in a white coat, looking down at him.

'So you are awake,' the doctor commented in broken English. 'Undo your pyjama jacket please.'

He did as he was instructed, noting the swabs of bandages wrapped around his stomach.

'What happened?' Sidney asked.

'You have a stomach wound, but you will be alright,' with that he wrote on a bed chart and turned to walk away.

'Doctor,' Sidney called.

'Yes,' he replied.

'Thank you.'

'Hmm,' the Doctor murmured, 'I suppose you should thank the soldier who didn't kill you.' With that he turned and walked away.

When he was fit Sidney was sent to a permanent camp at Stalag IXA.

The camp officer sat in the small room. He was engaged on one of the jobs that irked him, but was his responsibility to complete. Smoking British Goldflake he looked at the thin soldier standing in front of him.

'Name,' he asked stifling a yawn.

'Sidney Goldman.'

'Goldman. Sidney,' he typed on the personal card.

'Date and place of birth.'

'25 June 1919, London,' Sidney replied.

'Religion,' the bored officer asked, flicking the ash from his cigarette.

'Jew.'

'Jude – what did you say?'

'Jew. That is my religion.'

The officer stood up, his face red as he started screaming abuse at Goldman. The escort guard didn't understand what was going on. When Sidney answered in what was obviously a disrespectful manner by the way in which the officer reacted, the guard decided he should act and struck Sidney over the side of the head.

Once again when he recovered Sidney was lying on a bed; a soldier seeing him stir came up to him.

'I understand from the goon who brought you here that you are a Jew and proud of it.'

'Yea, that's right and they can stuff themselves if they think I am going to say different.'

'You don't understand do you?' the soldier replied. 'You will learn.' With that he walked away.

The weeks dragged by for Sidney, while every opportunity was taken to humiliate him by the guards who eventually gave him grudging respect. The Man of Confidence finally managed to get him transferred to the officer's camp at Spangenberg. The Senior British Officer Lt Colonel German knew of Sidney's situation and decided to make him his batman so he could give him some protection.

Guy German was not a man to sit still and had a reputation of encouraging escapes, stating it was every officer's duty. Eventually he was caught being involved in a tunnel escape and the Commandant, an old Prussian, saw an opportunity not only to get rid of German but also Goldman who he felt may not survive because of his religion. He did not want the responsibility of keeping him, just in case.

It was a cold dark night when the open lorry

carrying Guy German and Sidney Goldman approached Colditz Castle. German had invited Goldman to wear his spare greatcoat as it was cold and he didn't have one. On arrival at the castle Goldman jumped out dragging German's suitcase with him. A German officer stood there and saluted, 'Captain Priem,' he announced. 'The camp officer. Allow me.' With that he waved to a sentry to take the suitcase and turning led the way into the castle.

They entered the camp officer's room and he invited Goldman to sit down and in good English asked if he would like coffee.

'Thank you,' Goldman replied, accepting the cigarette that he was offered.

The door then opened and Colonel German entered holding Goldman's kitbag.

'Yours I believe Goldman?' He asked with a smile on his face having taken in the situation.

'Goldman! Goldman the Jew. You are not the Colonel?' Priem spluttered.

'No,' Sidney replied. 'I don't remember saying I was the Colonel.'

'That's enough Goldman,' German said. 'You had better be shown to your quarters, keep your mouth shut about this.' Then looking at Priem he remarked pointedly, 'We don't want to embarrass the Captain any further by letting this get out.'

The months passed and Sidney proved himself with the escape committee and Senior British Officer and he was the one they always called on for 'special jobs'. But he did suffer at the hands of the guards, although I understand this was never brought to the attention of the SBO or other officers. Within his own ranks, in particular the Poles, there was an understanding and whenever possible he was photographed so that people could see he was still alive.

On one occasion, once again involving Priem, four officers were suspected of escaping. Bursting into the orderlies' room Priem screamed at Sidney, 'Goldman, where have the British officers gone?'

'Oh that's nice,' Sidney replied. 'Do you think that whenever an officer wants to escape he comes up to me and says please Goldman may we leave?'

The other two orderlies in the room laughed.

Priem went red and shouted to the guards, 'Take the dogs up to the roof.'

'That's right,' retorted Sidney. 'They jumped off the roof — why don't you follow them?'

'Out, out all of you, out into the yard. You will stay there all night and if the officers are not found you will be shot.'

When the search was completed Priem returned to the yard with the guards. He saw Sidney standing in front of the orderlies handing each one a playing card, face down.

'Goldman, what are you doing?'

'Well Captain Priem, you said we are all going to be shot in the morning. To save you time we are deciding the order in which we will be shot. Highest card goes first.'

Priem's mouth gaped, the blood rushed to his face. He did not move. The guards looked terrified: the orderlies shifted their feet about and the laughter died on their lips. They had not seen Priem like this before. Sidney looked at Priem, this was it — he tensed as the German's hand went to his holster. It was empty — Sidney relaxed slightly, but only momentarily because Priem drew his dress sword and charged at him. Sidney turned and ran up the stairs to the orderlies' room and flung himself beneath a bunk. Priem exploded into the room and attacked the bunk with his sword, hacking it to pieces. Slowly his rage subsided: his chest heaved with the exertion as he turned and marched from the room.

There followed another period of solitary confinement for Sidney.

Sidney (back, second from left) endeavoured to be photographed whenever possible to prove he was not dead. The photograph is of Polish and British other ranks. Sidney told me he had just suffered a beating and had to be held up by two comrades for the picture to be taken.

Sidney seated between two Dutch officers at Colditz.

Dick Howe, the British escape officer wrote: "You refer to the late Solly Goldman with great affection, which I also share. One story concerning him might amuse you.

"Billie Stephens and Ronnie Littledale thought up the escape, which Pat Reid got home on. When they first discussed this with me, they had not carried out any reconnaissance on the German cookhouse where it was all going to start. Solly Goldman, very wisely, had appointed himself as chief British orderly in the cookhouse that he more or less ran in conjunction with a German unteroffizier whose name I cannot remember. I asked Solly to help me carry out

Sidney (seated, front right), at the hospital attached to Stalag IXC prior to repatriation. The photograph is stamped on the back by the Abwehr (security).

the reconnaissance at some time when the kitchen would be empty (we had our own keys). He told me that the German always went out between two and three in the afternoon, so it was arranged that I would pick the lock [using their crucible keys] and Solly would come with me to show me the geography of the place, which we as officers were not allowed into. At 2 o'clock on the due date I opened the locked door, which was supposed to be a sure sign that the German had gone. We were walking about inside, having locked the door behind us, when to my astonishment I turned into the German's sort of office area to see him fast asleep in a chair with his head cupped on his arms resting on a table. I made a move to retreat back through the main door which I started to reopen when I was nearly made to jump out of my skin. Solly, who was standing right in front of the German, let out a tremendous bellow of 'Achtung' [the German command for 'Attention'] which brought the German out of his chair in one leap, standing stiffly to attention. The German was naturally furious, but Solly gave him a lecture, in his appalling German, on the terrible state of the German Army and how mad Hitler would be if he ever heard about the way his troops went to sleep on duty. The resultant clatter and diversion gave me the cover I needed to open the door and slide out, whilst Solly emerged with the German telling him that if he wanted to go to sleep on duty why didn't he lock the door first. It was a superb piece of quick wittedness and needless to say we repeated the sortie a few days later, having got my 'stooges' to check that the German was not in the cookhouse.

"The Germans were not well disposed towards Sidney, even going to the lengths of removing his name from the repatriation list. However, the SBO brought this to the attention of the board and he was seen and repatriated in 1943."

Eggers wrote in 1970 that in his opinion Goldman was "the ace amongst the orderlies". He wrote asking me to persuade Sidney to write an article for his book but Sidney replied that, "The only good German....". Two years later I received a letter from his daughter who wrote that Sidney had died in his sleep on 3 June 1972.

On hearing of Solly's death Pat Reid wrote:

"Memory has dimmed the outline since the days of 1942 - now thirty years gone by — when Solly Goldman would be seen regularly in the early morning toting a steaming jug of ersatz coffee across the cobbled courtyard of Colditz towards the senior officers' quarters. Like all the orderlies and most of the officers imprisoned there, he wore wooden clogs on his feet and they clattered loud and clear like a football fan's rattle as he hurried towards the doorway and up the steep stone spiral staircase to the little cell where Colonel German, his devoted Senior British Officer, was roused and already shaving.

"I have had to turn up the pages of the Colditz story to remind myself of what I wrote about Solly in 1951 when I first put pen to paper to record the story of the fortress castle.

"His correct Christian name was Sidney but we usually called him Solly Goldman. He was an irrepressible London East End cockney with the lightning wit of the species. From his earliest years I am sure he learnt to get out of many a scrape by inducing gales of laughter in his tormentors. Now, in Germany, as an adult, he knew no other way. But his tormentors were Germans notable for their lack of any sense of humour. All he aroused in them was fury and being a self-confessed and more so a self-confident Jew, he heaped coals of fire upon his own head. He had the courage of a lion of Judah and no thought of self-pity for his tough lot ever entered his mind.

Photograph taken of Sidney in London after repatriation.

"And now, with a hard and tough life of breadwinning behind him, with the genuinely deserved easement of less arduous days ahead of him, after the turmoil and the struggle, fate it seems, in the form of the great reaper, has taken him away too soon.

"We, the men of Colditz, who all loved and admired his unquenchable humour and his dauntless spirit, wish him Godspeed wherever he may be and wherever he may go."

I gave this epitaph to *The Warren* for printing at the request of Pat Reid when he learnt of Solly's death.

Sidney Goldman (left), shown with other repatriates being greeted by the Mayoress of Stratford.

• THIRTEEN •
THE MUTINY DEATH SENTENCE

John Wilkins was a nodding acquaintance of mine for many months in the late sixties. He played the trumpet in a local public house on Sundays. One day I was invited to join John and his two fellow jazz musicians, who were brothers, for a pint. Conversation always centred on the pre-war jazz bands in which all three had played.

It was when I was involved in the BBC *Colditz* series at the beginning of the seventies, which I mentioned in conversation, that one of the two brothers told John to tell me his story of being a POW in Colditz.

It hit me like a thunderbolt: of course I had heard brief mention of the legend of the submariner named Wilkins sent to the castle under sentence of death for mutiny. That man was seated in front of me. I listened to his story, which he later repeated on tape during a visit to my home. This was stored in my Colditz collection until 2002 when it first appeared as an article for the Colditz Society magazine. This is that story.

"I was a boy entrant to the Navy in 1925 and went on subs in 1929. On 9 January 1940 I was the leading telegrapher on HMS *Starfish*. We were in the Heligoland after pilot boats. At 3am we saw a pilot cutter in the straits, and we went into attack even though the Germans were active in the area. The torpedo tube was fired but the torpedo didn't leave, however the air bubbles gave our position away. I counted over thirty-two depth charges dropped on us. We were on the bottom of eighty foot of water. The torpedo and engine rooms had taken water.

"At 4.30am the captain decided to raise to the surface, but we were stuck solid in mud at the front. Eventually we released ourselves and whilst rising to the surface heard a scraping sound on both sides of the hull. On breaking surface we were fired upon and had to abandon ship, it was freezing. The Germans had attached to a chain a buoy, with a red light one end and a white light the other end; when they saw the lights break surface they merely fired between the lights.

"We were all rescued from the sea and treated very well. The *Starfish* was towed into harbour; the third sub lost in three days. On arrival at Wilhelmshaven it looked like the whole German Navy was present, they lined the ships and saluted us. The snow lay thick on the docks and boarding plank. We marched smartly off the destroyer, when the worst possible thing happened, I slipped and fell face downwards in the snow and the whole German Navy cheered.

"After several moves I ended up at Marlag Nord in 1940 and was made Man of Confidence [Stalags had Men of Confidence rather than SBOs to liaise with the Germans, who were elected by the prisoners], because I was the most senior NCO who spoke German. Now to the question of mutiny. It happened like this. The Germans decided we should work on a Sunday. Under me was a hard crew of Eastenders who came from

John Wilkins with the author during a visit to record his experiences.

119

Forged pass given to Wilkins by Pat Reid in Colditz. Major Anderson took the photograph for the pass with his secret camera.

Rawalpindi. They ordered us to unload a lorry of stores going into an arms factory. I refused to allow this, as we were not going to help the German war effort on a Sunday or any other day. Rifles were pointed at us whereupon some of the Eastenders took them from the guards. I realised this was serious and ordered the men to return the rifles immediately. The guards seemed happy to let it drop and returned us to the barracks. I hoped this was the end of it but next day I was taken to Bad Sulza prison under escort and put in a cell. I was there six weeks during which every third day I received bread and water. During that time I witnessed a Frenchman taken into the office of the German corporal in charge where there was a lot of screaming followed by a shot. We never saw the Frenchman again.

"A man named Patterson from the American embassy kept in contact and told me I had been sentenced to death for mutiny. I was advised to get a German lawyer. He also supplied one from the American embassy.

"On 5 December 1940 I was taken under escort to Colditz. It was my wife's birthday. There were six other ranks present and once again they wanted me in charge.

"I remember one of them was Howard Gee, a civilian who was a suspect of the Germans. The other was a Jew named Solly Goldman; he was a plucky Eastender and didn't give a damn for the guards.

"Anyhow I refused to be in charge. Harry Elliott took me to Col German the SBO but I still refused. Then Eggers, who we called 'Vic Oliver', tried and on my refusal took me to the Commandant Schmidt. He was told I had not been sent as an orderly but as punishment. I asked why I had been sent to a special camp and not a work camp. He merely replied, 'You have been sent here,' making no further comment.

"I therefore acted as liaison between the officers and other ranks. Any trouble and they came to me. The castle didn't bother me, after Bad Sulza I could take anything. We only had one orderly who was a rebel and tried to stir things up with the other orderlies. He had a couple who would back him up, saying why should they work for the officers, they were prisoners the same as them. We nearly came to blows.

"Anyhow I became friends with a Dutchman, Tony Luteyn. We played together in the band. Because of my fluent German and my gear – I had a peak cap, navy jacket and trousers – I could easily pass in a disguise as the civilians that we were going to escape as. We were going to leave with the next group of civilian workmen. I got a false pass, worker's pass folder, and a map received in a record, all from Pat Reid. I was all prepared to go when I was taken ill and ended up in hospital. This was in 1941; I had been away six weeks and when I returned I found Tony had escaped with Airey Neave. This was a surprise and disappointment. I had arranged for a letter to be written for me which was supposed to be from a French woman who was to be my fiancée. Will Anderson took a photograph of me that was stuck on the forged pass. I was ready to go. The documents were kept inside the fur lining of my naval boots. They were never found.

"I managed with Dick Howe's help to get moved from Colditz to Lamsdorf. There I swapped places for a work party near a railway station. I left the job, walked to the station, bought a ticket and got on the train. Whilst there, there was a check and with some others I was taken from the train. I wasn't happy the way things were going and decided to tell them I was a POW and eventually I was returned to Lamsdorf.

"I never heard any more about my death sentence."

Map supplied by Pat Reid and carried by Wilkins in his escape from Lamsdorf camp.

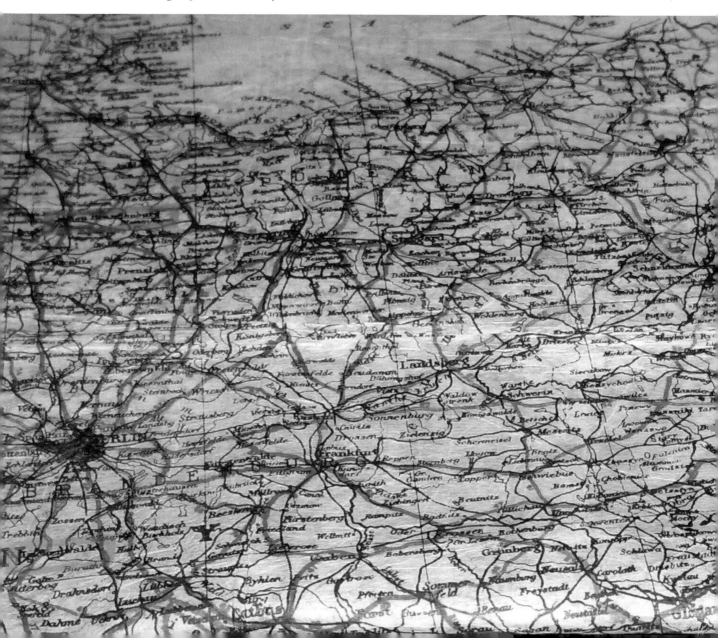

• FOURTEEN •
SECRETS OF THE COLDITZ HIDE AND RADIO ROOM

In January 1993 Reuters News Agency released a story throughout the Commonwealth together with America, France and Germany. Every national newspaper in Great Britain published it over a number of days. *The Daily Telegraph* used the headline 'Secrets of Colditz POW's radio room finally revealed'. It reported that during renovations of Colditz Castle, the workmen discovered a radio room untouched since 1945. It continued that a radio case, notebooks, pencils and electricity terminals for operating the radio, together with a series of sockets and light bulbs that were affixed to a back board, had been found.

What the media did not know was in fact this was the third time the radio room had been visited since the last war. The first occasion was in 1963 when Guigues, the Colditz French escape officer, had gone there with friends and relatives. Guigues had in fact originally constructed the radio room, his wife then smuggled the radio and components into Colditz through the use of 'explosive parcels' sent through the mail system. These were so named because if their contents were discovered everything would 'blow up' for those prisoners involved. When the French were moved from Colditz in 1943 Guigues bequeathed the radio room to Captain Dick Howe, the British escape officer. Dick wrote to me in the late sixties giving full details of the room itself.

I agreed to Reinhold Eggers' taking details from the letter on the radio room, for inclusion in a chapter in his book *Colditz Recaptured*. One part of the letter not used was the fact that an area outside the room was used as a 'hide' for storage of escape equipment and tools.

The second time the room was visited was in 1973. Four Colditz veterans — Rupert Barry, Jack Best, Dick Howe and Pat Reid — accompanied by Russell Miller of the *Radio Times* magazine, made a publicity trip to the castle in relation to the second TV series on Colditz. At that time it was situated in Eastern Germany and it took five weeks of negotiation before authority was obtained.

Knowing that Guigues had visited the radio room ten years earlier and found it intact, Dick decided to make this one of his prime destinations. When they reached the attic he pointed out to the others, who previously had no idea of the location of the radio room, the floorboard that acted as an entrance. Pulling the floorboard back he shone a torch down to reveal the room. Russell Miller volunteered to investigate. On entry Russell found Guigues had left everything covered in dust, just as it used to be. It is possible though that Guigues had removed some souvenirs including the radio valves as they were missing. Guigues would not however have known previously of the secret hide of escaping equipment. A dust-covered Russell acting on

The radio room now installed behind glass within the Colditz Museum.

123

Wall of the British quarters behind which the radio room was located. (My thanks to the Colditz Museum for authority to photograph the hide when first discovered.)

Signed cover of the *Radio Times* showing the secret radio hide artefacts.

instructions relayed by Dick removed a wealth of artefacts that were then taken to the courtyard for a photo shoot.

Amongst the items included were: a radio case, two notebooks of news transcripts, one notebook listing location of escape equipment and ownership, page to test forged rubber stamps, page of shorthand notes by Micky Burn of news transcripts, rushwoven basket of home-made screwdriver, nails, paint brush, razor blades, hacksaw, raincoat (stolen from dentist's waiting room), forged duplicated passes, two 1944 calendars etc. They were all brought back to England to feature in the exhibition on Colditz at the Imperial War Museum, which also included my collection. On 26 September 1974 I received a letter from Dick informing me he had no further use for the 'hide' which he donated to my collection.

Jimmy Yule wrote: "As far as the guts of the radio are concerned, I believe they were removed by some French visitors [Guigues] in the seventies or even in the sixties [1963] certainly before the visit of Dick Howe at the time of the TV programme. As far as I know I was the last to leave the cabin. I left everything intact and the place shipshape, with the notebooks on top of each other and the ash-tray, which we only used right at the end – for obvious reasons [the smoke would give them away] – on top of them."

Dick Howe wrote on the operation of the room: "When we inherited the radio room I was the receiver, whilst Micky Burn who knew shorthand took the notes. Later we had to have another team consisting of Jim Rogers, operator, and Jimmy Yule, scribe."

Describing the radio Jimmy Yule wrote: "I think it was a small Phillips manufactured in Eindhoven. A commercial radio you could buy off the shelf."

On messages Jimmy wrote: "Before reading the main news from London, the announcer, more often than not Mr Alvar Liddell, would read a number of short nonsensical sentences which meant something only to those who knew how to decode them. They were always short and sweet along the lines 'The milk has boiled over'. At no time was I asked to listen out for anything special, I don't think my partners Micky Burn or Jim Rogers were asked either." The phrases were in a previously arranged code to say something specific which would not have meant anything to the prisoners.

On the raincoat Yule wrote: "I rather fancy it must be the one Scorgie Price and Dick Howe liberated from the German dentist. Dick distracted the dentist by paying a huge bill in one mark lagergeld notes (POW money), long enough for Scorgie to rush behind the door and remove the coat from a hanger on a given signal. It was a very funny incident as it didn't work exactly to plan but in fact succeeded in the end."

In Pat Reid's book the coat is described as a grand affair with a fur collar. A case of poetic licence!

The Ausweis (travel permits) found in the hide were part of a reserve stock awaiting the

The power inputs for the radio.

The restricted area in which the radio was operated.

be used in an emergency to lower a man from the trapdoor within the radio room giving an exit in an emergency to the floor below. It was made from the blue and white bedding sheets that were issued to prisoners. This rope has unfortunately been rather cannibalised since it was found.

The two transcript books are full of news reports, doodles made during the long wait, maps etc, giving a snapshot of life in the radio hide. One book contained a page of doodles by Micky Burn. There is a drawing of a horse running towards a border with 'Well run old horse' referring of course to the news receiver Jim Rogers nicknamed 'Old Horse'. Another drawing is possibly a self-portrait of Burn to whom it has a slight resemblance from those days. Next to this are some Russian words, which Burn was studying at the time. There are some lyrics in one book, which Jimmy Yule wrote during slack moments for revues produced by Teddy Barton. The most famous is *Ballet Nonsense*, which the following poem is from.

HAS ANYBODY SEEN OUR SHIP?

What shall we do with the drunken sailor?
So the saying goes,
We're not tight but we're none too bright,
Great Scott! I don't suppose!
We've lost our way,
And we've lost our pay,
And to make the thing complete,
We've been and gone and lost the blooming fleet. (Repeat 1)

Has anyone seen our ship?
The HMS 'Peculiar',
We're been on shore,
For a month or more,
And when we see the captain we shall get what for,
Heave too my hearties,
Sing Glory Alleluia,
A lady bold as she could be,
Pinched our whistles at the Golden Flee,
Now we're in between the dark and the deep blue sea!
Has anyone seen our ship?

escapee's details and date to be filled in.

Will Anderson wrote: "It was customary to leave the filling in of the dates on passes until the very last possible moment before take-off, and even then a false start very often necessitated getting out a completely fresh set of papers. However, once the master copy of a pass had been done on the home-made duplicator, using Chivers' jellies from food parcels, and powdered ink from indelible pencils, it did not take too long to make new papers, and the escape officer built up a reserve to cover snap chance cases."

Bosun Chrisp of the Royal Navy, an expert on knots and rope making, made the radio room rope. The length was tied to a beam and was to

The radiomen Jimmy Yule and Jim Rogers (centre), with Pat Reid on the right. (*D. Ray*)

Here is a second poem found in the notebooks:

MAN ABOUT TOWN

We're two chaps who,
Find it thrilling,
To do the killing,
We're always willing,
To give the girls a treat,
Just a drink at the Ritz,
Call it double or quits,
Then we feel the world is at our feet,
Top hats, white spats,
Look divine on us,
There's a shine on us,
Get a line on us,
When we come your way,
God! Eleven o'clock!
Let's pop into the Troc,
Ere we start the business of the day.

After the lyric above there are copies of news items; it does not state who the speaker is. It looks to be a partial copy of an American propaganda broadcast: "Dear America richer than any other, humanitarians, scientists, partnership formed workers, businessmen. Material standard of living scale. Average wage appears to attract the most. I formed the commitment at home of total victory. Forward in faith, driving spirit of USA."

The rest consists mainly of war news with a sprinkling of home news. For example: "Oxford. University Oxford and Cambridge will have boat race probably on last Saturday in February. Oxford won race last February at Ely and have their turn to arrange. No Young or Johnson who rowed boat last race."

"1944. June 6. Hold positions W.Caen. 16.55 Von R reports this evening it is the Führer's explicit desire for Dilmon, Rommel, Döniz."

"June 11. Marcke. Picture of internal

disputes, failure of Germans to hold together. C of staff situation near Avranches very unclear. Air superiority stupendous. French underground patriots growing braver. Same conditions in Holland today as in Normandy 3,000 aeroplanes and gliders. Other ops. Landing in Holland. 21,000 time bombs dropped in 20 mins loss of only two bombers."

Getting wartime access to the radio room and hide had to be very systematic. The door to the attic was unlocked, and then a 'stooge' bent down to see if any items had been placed on the floor. For example on one occassion when entering the loft Guigues saw a piece of blank paper. He left it there. Suddenly guards made a surprise visit and he hid in the rafters. Thankfully the guards didn't look up or they would have seen him. They were concentrating on the floor and bent down to pick up the paper, placing it in another spot and measuring it from the wall. Obviously to try to set a trap to see if anyone had been in the loft.

Guigues passed this information on plus the fact that any dust disturbed had to be replaced.

Therefore the 'stooge' would note how the loft looked. He would replace the floorboard after the radio team had entered the hide. Dust was laid and the loft door locked. A warning light in the radio room indicated if there was any danger. It also indicated when it was time to leave and the floorboard would be opened.

The radio table consisted of a door taken from a toilet. There were two stools and blankets covered the walls to muffle any sound. The actual room itself was located behind the wall on the third floor occupied by the British after the French had left. A bunk was against the dividing wall, the occupant never knowing that the radio room was so close and being used at 7pm every night.

On one occasion Micky Burn discovered a page of notes he had taken in shorthand to read out were missing. He sweated that he had dropped it in the loft and lay sleepless all night wandering if he had given the radio room away. He decided not to mention it in case of a panic. Next day he made sure he was the first to enter the loft and found the page lying near the door. With relief he scooped it up without being seen.

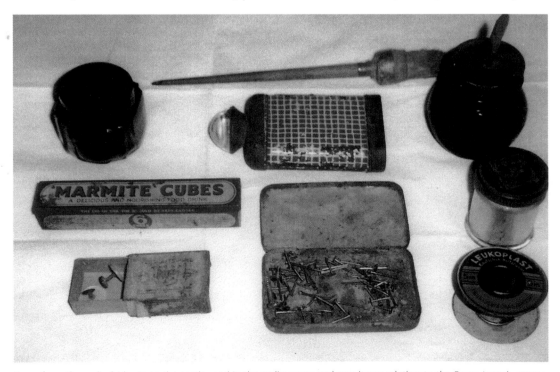

Items from the radio hide. Note the torch used in the radio room and two items relating to the Franz Joseph escape – the paintbrush used to paint the cap and the silver paint tin (centre right), used for the badge.

Apart from building the glider, the radio room and hide constituted the most dangerous occupation at Colditz. One little mystery remains today, however.

In the book *Detour*, there is a small photograph of Dick Howe wearing earphones, seated at the radio. The caption reads, "The photograph was taken on the day of liberation by Michael Burn with a camera he purchased from the Germans for cigarettes."

I contacted Michael Burn on the subject, as I was troubled by the radio shown in the picture. He replied that he did in fact pay 200 cigarettes to Will Anderson for a camera he had obtained from a German. Burn then went on to say that he took snaps around the castle on liberation day, as he wanted the film sent to the *Times*. This was to supplement the report he had written on the liberation. The report in fact appeared in the *Times* on 21 April 1945, but without any pictures. I pointed out to Michael that there had been no pictures and asked if he knew what happened to the film. His reply was that he had asked a GI to send it back to England for him but it had not been seen since.

This account fails to explain two questions regarding the photograph credited to Burn in the book. The first is where did this come from if the film disappeared, and secondly the radio shown is not the same as the case found in the hide by Howe during the *Radio Times* visit.

Yule remembers the radio having a Phillips case, which is the one found in the hide. Therefore it is possible that the photograph shows the second radio, as it is known there was one French and one English radio. The French radio was taken into the courtyard after the photograph was taken. I have been informed that news bulletins and music were heard in the yard on liberation day.

It would explain the differences in the radio cases. As far as the missing film and the appearance of the photograph, the explanation could be as follows. Jerry Wood, the author of *Detour*, had planned the book prior to Colditz being liberated. The photographs would be useful for the book. As the radio one appeared credited to Burn it must be from the missing film. However, no other pictures from the film have appeared.

The suggestion therefore is that the film did arrive in London and Jerry, knowing of its destination, managed to obtain just the one copy for his book. It is of course possible he received the other prints from the film but this is doubtful, as they would have surfaced at some future date, unless of course they are in some private collection or museum. The mystery may never be solved.

The unanswered letter included these words,

The radio hide on display at the 'Escape' exhibition at the Imperial War Museum, 2004/05. Note: Phillips radio case, escape rope, notebooks for messages, the 'dentist's' raincoat, and cigarette packets containing German money.

• FIFTEEN •
THE COLDITZ GLIDER

Colonel Tod received a letter on 12 May 1971. This had been written by Reinhold Eggers, who as a captain of the Wehrmacht had been responsible for the security at Colditz Castle during the latter part of the war. The purpose of the letter was to try and persuade the Colonel, the Senior British Officer from 1943 until liberation in 1945, to supply a chapter for Eggers' proposed book.

"my biggest defeat was being shown a photograph of the glider and of its construction in the Colditz loft. Then to learn that two civilians supplied tools. All this during the last year of the war when I was in charge of security."

It may have been Eggers' biggest defeat but for the men of Colditz the glider named the Colditz 'Cock', changed in later years to the 'Spirit of Colditz', encapsulated perfectly the endless battle by men imprisoned, but not defeated. Tony Rolt, a pre-war Goodwood motor racing champion, first voiced the glider idea in 1944. He discussed this with Bill Goldfinch who already had similar thoughts of escape. Jack Best, an escaping partner of Bill's, joined the team together with Lorne Welch, a

The 'Mole Men of Sagan'. A team of three men consisted of Bill Goldfinch, (second left), Jack Best to the right, and Henry Lamond at the extreme right. These men dug a 'blitz' tunnel close to the wire and just below the surface. After entering the tunnel was filled and air holes were made as they progressed successfully beneath the wire and escaped. On recapture Best and Goldfinch were sent to Colditz where they were involved in building the glider. On the left is Dicky Edge.

The surviving tools used for making the glider. Now held at the Imperial War Museum.

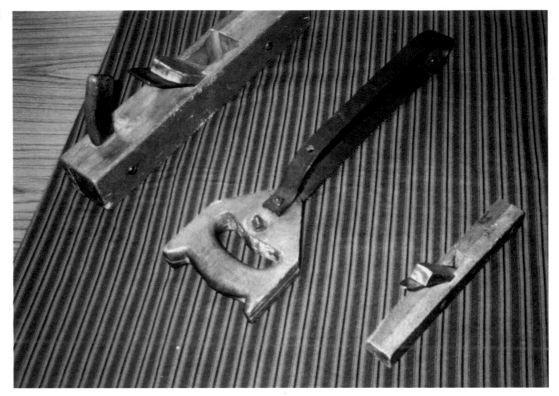

gliding expert. With Tony Rolt in charge, Bill on design and Jack and Lorne on construction, an escape was planned.

Colonel Tod, the SBO, on being informed of the idea of the glider agreed with the escape committee to it being built on condition that when completed the glider would only be used on his authority. Tod felt that the chances were that when the Germans lost the war, which in his opinion was inevitable, the inmates of Colditz had little chance of survival. They thought there were SS in the town, who would 'deal' with the prisoners at the end of the war. With the arrival of Colonel Stirling, the founder of the Long Range Desert Group and father of the SAS, he had a fighting leader who was charged with forming a defence group. It was planned that the men of Colditz would die fighting.

Therefore Tod informed his committee and the glider group that the glider would only be used to obtain help from advancing allies should it become obvious the prisoners were in mortal danger. Two of the four-man team would be

used to fly the craft. There was a real danger of course that building the glider could also jeopardise the radio room as the only suitable place for it to be built was in the radio room loft. A false wall was constructed at one end of the long room with a trapdoor entrance.

The loft being empty, the gamble was that guards would not bother to walk the full length of the dark room. Distributing dust on the floor would prevent them from knowing if anyone had entered the loft. The guards restricted their inspection to the immediate area of the door, so that if there had been any entry into the loft it would be immediately spotted.

Jack Best wrote in August 1997: "A goon that we called 'Slim' was an odd type on general and masonry/plaster work. He was originally in uniform and then became a civilian. He came to me very excited one day; my German is almost nil but it was obvious that he had found the trapdoor in the ceiling to get into the glider workshop. I don't think he had seen the glider; but I immediately got Chalupka, who worked 'Slim' amongst many others. Later Chalupka told me not to worry as he had bought him off with 700 cigarettes. I still find it difficult to realise that a bribed German always kept his word to Chalupka. He almost certainly had something thank goodness; although only a sergeant, he had posed as an officer. I do not know what we would have done without him. [The fact is that Chalupka thought it would be to everyone's advantage if he posed as an officer, as the other Czech airmen were sergeants. A select few were told of the true rank, and Bader guessed it.] Douglas Bader knew his real rank; but no one else as far as I know until after the war. It is true that Slim died two weeks later; but he had got diabetes and that was why he was a civilian. I must say I felt better when we heard he had died."

The late Skelly Ginn kindly gave me a copy of his excellent article 'From Maginot Line to Colditz' in response to my request for information on the glider. Included are the following observations: "This was constructed, along with some other interesting projects, in a secret workshop built amongst the roof trusses of the highest and longest wing. An artificial wall was built on a truss 4 metres from the outer gable wall. The main spars of the glider came from specially selected long, sound floor planks quietly replaced by shorter lengths from less noticeable places.

"The multitude of the light ribs were carved and glued to detail drawings. The wings and body were covered with bedding material doped with some waxy mess made from oats or millet from the cookhouse. Aileron hinges and other metal parts came from locker and door fittings and were my responsibility. It is surprisingly difficult making drilling tools – or even a decent hammer from scratch. For blacksmith work forges were made by fixing food tins into one another to create an up draught, but for efficiency it was necessary to duct the incoming air so that it became preheated before combustion.

"The carpenter's most useful tool was a bow saw with a blade formed from a gramophone main spring. Of course all this sort of activity had to be 'stooged'. Watchers in convenient positions would have two or three different books to read, or different shaped objects would appear on a certain windowsill. Invariably whenever a German officer entered the camp, he would be preceded by shouts of 'goons up'."

Dr Charles Hutt gave some verse to Bill Goldfinch after a spell of 'stooging' for the glider. It is reproduced overleaf in full.

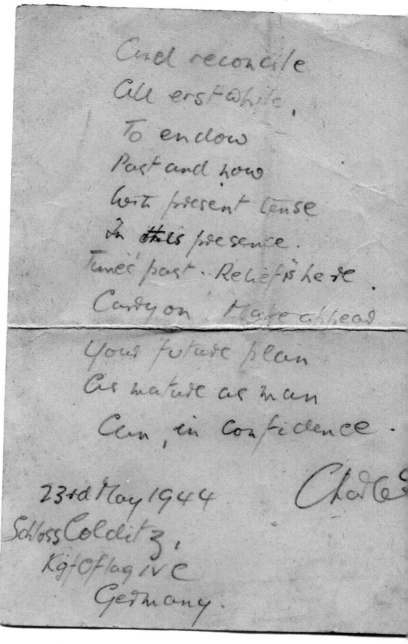

Part of the verse written by Dr Hutt after stooging (being lookout) on glider duty.

To Jack Best and Bill Goldfinch as a tribute to their active spirit

They said on stooging I couldn't learn verse
Would it I wonder make me totally immerse?
Myself in the prospect of what's been and done,
Lose present senses as when a song
Is being sung of Alice has gone
Or before, and is never o'er
Or would I see no enemy
Have to mind nearly blind
To memory
Should it not heighten our intent –
Let nothing relent our discontent
Herein to be pent
Release our sense
Of permanence
And reconcile
All erstwhile,
To endow
Past and now
With present tense,
In this presence
Times past. Relief is here
Carry on. Make appear
Your future plan
As mature as man,
Can, in confidence.

23 May 1944, Schloss Colditz, Kgf Oflag IVC, Germany
Charles Hutt

Skelly continues: "The glider launch was to have been from a wooden guard rail on a roof ridge, out of sight of the ground, and the 'catapult' powered by a tin bath full of earth and stones, released from a top floor window, pulling a rope made from parcel string – incidentally, 'rope walks' were an essential manufacturing feature of all camps at some time! The clatter of the falling tin bath was expected to make sentries look down rather than up, so on a dark night the pilot, with one other, could dive and get the feel

Lorne Welch, who was a British glider champion with his wife Ann. With Best and Goldfinch he joined Tony Rolt (Goodwood motor champion) in building the glider.

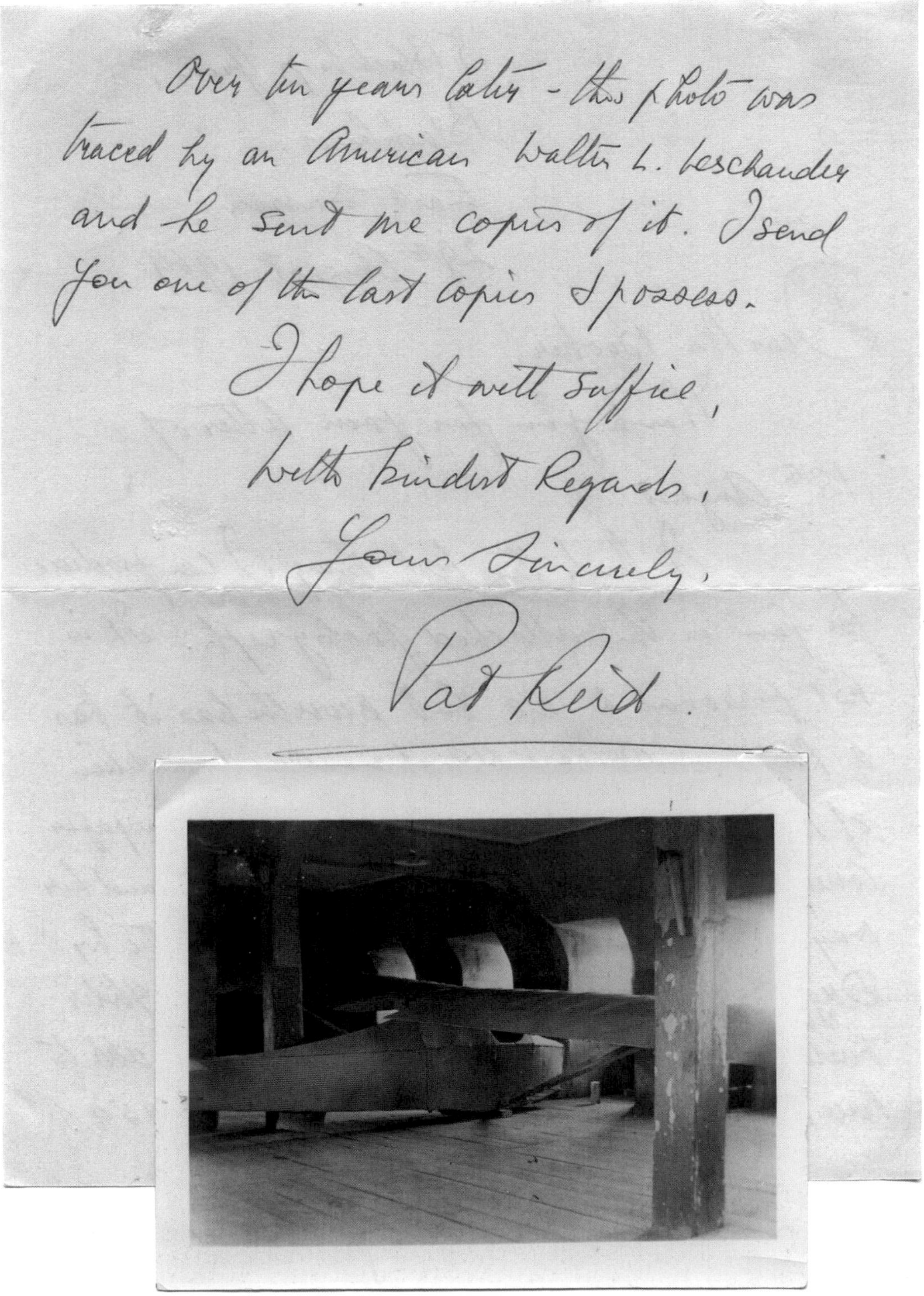

Over ten years later – this photo was traced by an American Walter L. Leschander and he sent me copies of it. I send you one of the last copies I possess.

I hope it will suffice,

With kindest Regards,

Yours Sincerely,

Pat Reid.

Letter from Pat Reid with a copy of one of the last original photographs of the glider.

The roof of Colditz Castle from where the glider would be launched. The proposed landing ground was beyond the River Mulde.

of the controls in time to make a soft landing in the river 300 feet below."

Bill Goldfinch wrote in 2001 in response to a letter in which I asked about a photograph I had seen allegedly of a wheel for the glider. Could it in fact have been a pulley of some kind?

"Regards how big the 'wheel' is! A control cable pulley would be approx 2 inches diameter with a groove for the cable – the launching trolley [never constructed] would have had about a 12 inch diameter – the glider had only a keel and skid."

In the event it was not necessary to use the glider. Although the Prominente were forced to move under escort the only SS units available to 'deal' with the prisoners were the concentration camp guards at a nearby camp for Jews. They were not front line troops as camp guards were mainly 'rejects' and towards the end consisted of anti-Semitic mercenary forces from occupied countries.

Master Sergeant Genz, the Commandant of the concentration camp merely wanted to take the Colditz men with the remains of his Jewish prisoners. He was under the false impression they would be cowed prisoners. Tod had by now an effective defence force and warned Prawitt they would not move. Prawitt managed to arrange a delay in the order and the concentration camp victims left with the guards on their murderous journey to Theresienstadt.

On 16 April 1945 the American liberators entered Colditz and the castle, and during the first few hours the glider was the source of amazement to the conquering heroes.

PFC Robert Hoffman of anti-tank platoon HQ 3 Bn 273rd Inf. Regt. wrote: "I saw the glider a week after the liberation of the castle. It was assembled in the castle attic and I was able to examine it close up. I was amazed at the construction, covered expertly with blue checked cloth. The central line pulleys were carved and look to function properly."

1st Lt. Kent of HQ Co 3 Bn: "Spent most of my time with the English officers who showed me the glider. Had a few snapshots taken of it but have given them away."

The questions always asked are what happened to the glider and would it have flown?

To the first question the probable answer is that it was broken up for firewood. Being so close to the eastern borders, the town was swarming with refugees, comprised of forced labour workers returning home and volksdeutch expelled from their homes returning to relatives in Germany. The castle was the only large building able to accommodate the masses. One of the coldest winters on record at that time meant that firewood was at a premium and the Russians having no interest in the glider would not have heeded to its destruction.

To the second question the answer is a resounding 'yes'. The glider expert Martin Francis had built a quarter-scale model from the original plans, which flew. Later his knowledge and the expertise of a manufacturer built a full-scale model for a television programme and on Wednesday 2 February 2000 at 12.30pm in the grounds of the high security RAF station at Odiham in Hampshire, the 'Spirit of Colditz' floated gently across the cloudless sky.

Many Colditz veterans were present including Jack Best and Bill Goldfinch. A happy ending to an ambitious and brave escape enterprise, surely worthy of the men and spirit of Colditz.

A scale working model of the glider built to the original plans by Martin Francis (centre) with Jack Best on the left, and Bill Goldfinch on the right. (*M. Francis*)

SIXTEEN

THE UNSEEN HEROES

Seven handcuffed commandos were led from their cells at the RSHA (Reich security forces) headquarters in Berlin. The guards handed them over to their escort of four SS soldiers with a senior sergeant in charge. They were led to a prison bus waiting in the quadrangle of the building. Once on board they sat separately on wooden seats with two guards front and rear.

The commandos noted the black-painted barred windows, and the metal door that divided the body of the bus from the driver's compartment. The sergeant who then sat with the driver locked this. They were the only two that knew the destination of the bus.

The date was 7 October 1942.

The bus was driven eastwards from Berlin at a leisurely pace. The driver knew he was not scheduled to return until the following day. Aware that escape was not possible, the commandos decided to relax during the time they had alone. Some with eyes closed ran through the operation that had brought them to their current situation.

It was 16 September 1942 when the commando team led by Captain Black and Captain Haughton, with ten other ranks including two Norwegians, had landed on the coast of Norway. Transported by the French submarine *Junon*, their operation, codenamed 'Musketoon', was to blow up the heavy water factory at Glomfjord.

Led by Sgt O'Brien, the senior NCO, who was a mountain climber and veteran of the St Nazaire raid, it took them a day to negotiate the glaciers, snow and ice plains before reaching the target area. They then rested and after a brief meal found shelter and bedded down for the night in their sleeping bags.

The following day Black and two men negotiated the target and came across their first obstacle. Neither the intelligence reports nor air reconnaissance had revealed that a deep valley lay between them and the heavy water factory. Also there was no road that they could use, so they had no alternative but to scale down the valley and up the other side. There were exposed areas on the opposite side of the valley, which would have to be climbed at night.

Returning to camp they reported their findings and made their plans. Food would be their main problem, as at least a day would be added to the operation. The following day they all returned to the valley, which they were able to descend, then they rested until nightfall. As soon as it was dark they began the hazardous climb up the valley, once more led by O'Brien. Then they were hampered by torrential rain, which was

The area of the deep valley negotiated by the Musketoon commandos.

Right: Rifleman Cyril Abram photographed two months before the mission. He was later shot.

Far right: Lance Sergeant Chudley photographed on enlistment.

good for cover but it curtailed their progress and daylight came before they were halfway up which meant they were in danger of being revealed. The only shelter they could find were a number of boulders with a flat rock area; it was still raining heavily and they were soaked to the skin and not able to risk a fire.

Black decided they would stay there that day and make it their camp. That night they would complete the climb and attack the factory. It was now 20 September.

The operation was planned with two teams. O'Brien would lead the first with Chudley and Curtis, their job being to blow up the pipelines. The second team with the remainder of the commandos led by Captain Black would attack the factory.

And so the assault began. O'Brien and his team laid the explosives without any problems and waited for the flashlight signal to set the half-

hour fuses. On arrival at the factory the two Norwegian commandos were sent in to clear the factory of civilian workers and to check if any Germans were present.

Once the factory was cleared the explosives were set and detonated. On seeing the factory erupt O'Brien set the fuses for the pipeline and they made their escape. The nearby German garrison was soon in pursuit of the saboteurs. The factory team had learnt of a bridge that crossed a mountain pass but in the dark the first commandos to arrive missed the steps. They made for a large hut to get directions or ask for a guide, and find if any Germans were in the area. Learning there were no Germans or anyone willing to act as a guide, they departed having received some directions.

As they left two Germans arrived from the other end of the hut, looking for the commandos. It was then that Haughton and the

Norwegian commando Djupdraet arrived. A fight ensued during which a German fled and the other was killed; Djupdraet was bayoneted which later proved fatal. In the meantime the commandos had met up in two groups. In the first were O'Brien, Trigg, Fairclough and Granlund; the remainder joined up with the second group. This second group made for their camp to collect provisions and continue their escape. Unfortunately the Germans had found it and were waiting in ambush. A battle took place during which Haughton was shot in the arm. Superior forces in numbers and firepower overpowered them.

Now, as prisoners, the commandos were aware the bus was driving down a steep hill before sweeping left, then right, over a bridge. They then felt it climb a cobbled street before making a five-point turn to climb a further gradient and stop.

The senior sergeant left the bus and walked to the main gate of the castle. A guard led him into the arched entrance, where the sergeant of the guard, on reading the documents produced, called the camp duty officer. He in turn took the documents to the Commandant's private quarters.

The Commandant Colonel Glaesche telephoned OKW headquarters in Dresden. He was instructed that the commandos were not in any circumstances to have contact with the other prisoners. They were only to be held there temporarily until a decision was made on their future. Glaesche instructed the duty officer to escort the prison bus to the arrest house. This was located in Colditz town, a short distance from the castle. This building was formerly the town jail and was used as an overflow prison for POWs held in solitary confinement. It was under the control of Corporal Reichmann, a member of Eggers' Colditz security team.

The commandos were held in cells on the top floor of the two-storey building. Both the prison bus and escort were then released from their duty.

Eggers wrote in his diary:

"7 October 1942. Seven soldiers arrived but we had no order from the OKW to accept them at Colditz and Colonel Glaesche refused to allow them into the camp."

Captain Dick Howe, the escape officer, reported to Colonel 'Daddy' Stayner, the Senior British Officer: "G has told Checko that seven commandos are in the arrest house. He has no names but believes they are only here temporarily."[1]

Stayner replied: "Right, get Goldman to take breakfast to our men in solitary at the arrest house. Get the names of the commandos and any other information. We will get Rupert to send it back to War house."[2]

The following morning Goldman went to see Stayner with Howe, saying, "It's no good, those guys are keeping their lips sealed. They are a hard bunch, relaxed but not giving anything away in case I am a stooley. I need something to impress them I am genuine."

"Right Dick," Stayner instructed, "have a word with one of the men who have done commando training and get their advice on the best way to convince them."

They were successful and in a 1971 letter Goldman wrote:

"I was the last person to see the commandos alive and I didn't know until Schofield [Stephen Schofield, author of the book *Musketoon*] told me that they had been shot. I sure was upset to hear same as I got along real fine with them after they found out who I was and trusted me. Still that's what war was all about."

Eggers in a letter dated 2/12/69: "I saw Haughton and the commandos. I well remember the men in their camouflage dress. They had no badges of rank. At Colditz the men did not suffer. The commandos behaved themselves, if they hadn't they would have been court marshalled and legally shot."

---

1. 'Checko' was the nickname of Chalupka. He was given sole control of bribery and corruption, at which he was highly successful. 'G' is one of the names given by Eggers to Tod in a letter dated 1971 giving names of German suspects.
2. Rupert refers to Captain Rupert Barry. War house was the common name used by POWs for the War Office.

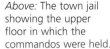
Above: The town jail showing the upper floor in which the commandos were held.

Above right: A photograph of the town jail entrance taken by the author in 1980. It is identical to the Haughton photograph of 1942 (see opposite).

Eggers also wrote: "The prison bus and guards had left soon after they arrived. Train would most likely have returned the 'Norwegian' commandos to Berlin. But I have no knowledge of this."

The secrecy surrounding the commandos at Colditz was such that it was not known if they were to stay there. Therefore Lange, the castle photographer who made a profitable business of selling prints to the prisoners, carried out the normal procedure of photographing the prisoners. They were snapped on the entrance steps and side wall of the arrest house.

On 13 October the Gestapo won their battle with the OKW over control of the men. In the knowledge of Hitler's instruction on the 'Commando Order' (known as the 'Bullet Order' where all commandos and saboteurs after interrogation were to be shot), the Gestapo reclaimed them. The order was issued in Germany on 18 October 1942.

They were returned to Gestapo HQ in Berlin for extensive interrogation. On 22 October they again left under escort in a prison bus. This time the trip was much shorter and they arrived at Sachsenhausen concentration camp in the suburbs of Berlin. Here, they were taken directly to the Zellerbau cells outside the main camp area. At dawn the following morning 1st Lieutenant SS Doctor Heinze Baumkotter took them for a medical examination. After the initial check they were taken individually to a rear area of the building to record their height and weight. Whilst stood against the wall for a height check with a measuring stick they were shot in the back of the neck. Death would have been instantaneous.

Shot at Sachsenhausen were: Captain Graeme Black, Captain Joseph Haughton, C.S.M Miller Smith, L/Sgt William Chudley, Pte Reginald Makeham, Rflm Cyril Abram, Pte Eric Curtis.

Corporal Sverre Granlund returned to England via Norway. He was drowned in February 1943 when a submarine in which he was travelling to another operation was sunk. Private Fred Trigg, who returned via Sweden, was killed in action in Italy. Sgt Richard O'Brien, who returned via Spain and Gibraltar, survived the war. Corporal John Fairclough, who returned via Sweden, also survived the war. Corporal Erling Djupdraet died of wounds in a Norwegian hospital.

The captured Musketoon men were not taken to the castle until a decision was made on their future. They were held in the town jail where they were individually photographed outside the main entrance. Shown here is the one taken of Captain Haughton.

Identity pass issued to Sergeant O'Brien in Gibraltar after his evasion and eventual escape to England.

• SEVENTEEN •
RESCUE OF THE AMERICAN OSS AND 'ALBANIAN' COMMANDOS OF COLDITZ

In September 1969 Reinhold Eggers, the chief security officer at Colditz, wrote to me one of his long and informative letters. Enclosed was a five-page report, closely typed. Eggers explained that Mr Rudolf Denzler, the Swiss representative for Colditz, had given the report to Eggers who in turn was forwarding it to me.

The report explained how Denzler joined the Swiss legation in Berlin in the summer of 1943. He acted as Protecting Power for the United States of America, the British Empire and several minor states. His duties were reporting on visits to POW camps and hospitals.

In July 1944 Denzler was on a routine visit to the POW camp at Kaisersteinbrück. An OKW officer Major Richard Romer accompanied him, a professor in civilian life and personal friend of Denzler. Their visit was to an international camp and was to the British section that held about three hundred other ranks.

Everything appeared to be in order but then the British Man of Confidence (a senior NCO who spoke German) approached Denzler when he was alone. He was told that British uniforms had been seen in the convict section at the end of the camp. There was always a conference at the end of a visit, over which the Commandant presided. Denzler asked to see the British prisoners in the convict section. The Austrian Commandant, a colonel, was taken by surprise at the request and with embarrassment turned to

the OKW major for support. The major stood up and said, "The representative of the Swiss Government has the right to go wherever British men are detained, we have nothing to conceal."

Whilst he walked to the end of the camp, Denzler was assured by the Commandant that he had no commanding authority over these particular prisoners, they were simply lodged within his security system.

An inspection found seven British subjects in solitary confinement. These were Brigadier General E.F. Davies, Captains Vercoe, Hawkesworth and Watts, and NCOs Gray, Shenton and Robinson. This team had been parachuted into Albania on a commando mission; they were captured on 13 January 1944. Some of them were wounded. At first held by the German Army, they had been handed on 31 March to the SD, a Security Service of the SS and Gestapo. The prisoners were then badly treated under interrogation at the Gestapo jails of Belgrade, Mauthausen and Vienna. Then on 7 June they were moved to the convict section of their present camp.

Denzler decided to examine the whole convict section and on going from cell to cell also found in solitary confinement four American citizens, namely Colonel Florimond Duke, Captains Nunn and Suarez, and an American major of Yugoslav descent.

Colonel Duke and the captains had landed by parachute into Hungary on 15 March 1944. Invited by the Horthy Government Duke had been appointed an Extraordinary Envoy and entrusted with a high level political mission. The Gestapo already being well established in Hungary, they arrested Duke and his companions and the mission failed. Had it succeeded a different chapter may have been added to the history of World War Two.

For all their sufferings Denzler reported that the men were in excellent military deportment and their morale was unshaken. The OKW officer began to explain why their circumstances were different to other prisoners of war. The allied commando raids on the French coast and Norway had so enraged Hitler that he personally evolved on 18 October 1942 a top-secret order, as we have seen earlier. In brief all commando prisoners, in or out of uniform were to be dealt with first by interrogation and then shot. The Army was to hand over all such prisoners to the security services.

The first victims were the Musketoon raiders who were executed on 23 October 1942 (see pages 139-143). Denzler also reported that fifteen Americans, all in uniform, who landed on a commando mission in the Balkans, were executed in January 1945, in Mauthausen, Austria.

In consideration of the gravity of the situation, Major Romer broke off the journey and returned to headquarters, the prisoner-of-war division, OKW – German High Command, in Torgau. Head of this division was General Westhoff, a straightforward officer. Denzler had found the General a friendly and agreeable man throughout his contact with him.

General Westhoff requested the RSHA (Reich Security Central Office) surrender the seven Britons and four Americans to the jurisdiction and custody of the Army. He had a good hand to play with; the fact that the Swiss Protecting Power was aware of the existence and whereabouts of these men was surely helpful.

This became a fact on 23 August 1944, when the men arrived at Oflag IVC in Colditz. A week later Denzler paid a routine visit to the camp and was pleased to meet them under happier surroundings. On this occasion, he entered in his notebook a statement from Brigadier Davies:

"Before we left [Kaisersteinbrück] they allowed us to wash our clothes. We left on 20 August; a special Gestapo jailer came to chain us in pairs for the journey. I was chained to Colonel Duke, USA, we travelled in one third of a cattle truck, and the weather was hot and conditions most unpleasant. We arrived at the Schloss chained up.

"The moment we stripped off their handcuffs in the courtyard of Colditz, we became conventional prisoners well protected by the Geneva Convention of 1929, the lawful status that had been so wrongfully denied to us for several months."

Kenneth Lockwood reports on the entrance of Colonel Duke:

"I was stooging at the top of the castle looking down into the German yard when I saw this officer, wearing a leather flying jacket with a fur collar. He had a flat cap on and wore a moustache. He was talking to Eggers and was alone. I said afterwards to some of the chaps that I thought I had seen a Yank enter the courtyard and sure enough I later found out it was Duke."

Although the group was still under the eyes of the SD, thanks to Denzler they survived the war.

CAHIERS D'ÉTUDES EUROPÉ...

CAHIERS D'ÉTUDES EUROPÉENNES

A PATRIOT...

How ODD...

MY ALLY

BY

Winston Churchill

ENGLAND FACES EUROPE

JOHN AMERY

THE SOVIETS ARE THEY HUMAN?

· EIGHTEEN ·
THE BRITISH FREE CORPS
AT COLDITZ

The British Free Corps, formed in 1944, were a hotchpotch group of opportunists; some had been pre-war members of the Mosley Party, whilst others were swayed by intimidation. Apart from a few anti-Semitic, anti-Communist fanatics, they had no intention of laying down their lives for Germany. The unit was never larger in size than a platoon.

Eggers records in his diary for June 1944:
"Two men from the 'British Legion', known as the British Free Corps, walked into the Commandant's office. The men were dressed in blue uniform [boiler suits] with armbands bearing BFC. They produced papers from the OKW. These stated they had authority to visit all POW camps to recruit for the BFC. I had been on a two-day propaganda course near Zossin in Berlin when they spoke of recruiting to the Legions. There were 'Wlassow' there and they talked of recruiting British officers from Colditz. Now they were here. I thought it was either a bad joke or a complicated escape plan. I immediately telephoned the OKW and was told that they were genuine and were to be given every assistance. They produced leaflets and some small books for recruitment and propaganda. They wanted to interview recruits and give a presentation to the camp. [These visits to camps had dismal results for the effort involved.]

"I warned the Commandant that not only would there be no recruits but the danger of a lot of trouble for us and a real danger to the two men. We eventually convinced the recruiters to leave a stack of leaflets and booklets instead. They were placed in the prisoners' mail and I put one on the officers' mess board. The booklets were also left in the prisoners' canteen where other propaganda material was situated. However the SBO Colonel Tod complained about the leaflets which called on the officers to break their oath to King and country. He ordered they should all be burnt in the prisoners' yard. I was asked afterwards for souvenirs, but they were all gone and I removed the one from the officers' mess."

Some of the titles of the booklets are as follows.

A Patriot Speaks: the author is described as 'a retired captain of the British Army who remains anonymous until free speech is permitted'.

The Big Jews and the Smaller Jews in Mr Roosevelt's Administrative Body.

The Soviets Are They Human?

The Axis Powers Are Stronger Than Their Opponents.

As a result of repeated applications from British subjects from all parts of the world wishing to take part in the common European struggle against Bolshevism authorisation has recently been given for the creation of a British volunteer unit.

The British Free Corps publishes herewith the following short statement of the aims and principles of the unit.

1) The British Free Corps is a thoroughly British volunteer unit, conceived and created by British subjects from all parts of the Empire who have taken up arms and pledged their lives in the common European struggle against Soviet Russia.

2) The British Free Corps condemns the war with Germany and the sacrifice of British blood in the interests of Jewry and International Finance, and regards this conflict as a fundamental betrayal of the British People and British imperial interests.

3) The British Free Corps desires the establishment of peace in Europe, the development of close friendly relations between England and Germany, and the encouragement of mutual understanding and collaboration between the two great Germanic peoples.

4) The British Free Corps will neither make war against Britain or the British Crown, nor support any action or policy detrimental to the interests of the British People.

Published by the British Free Corps

The leaflet removed from the officers' mess by Eggers.

Booklets distributed by the BFC during their visit to Colditz.

F/LT Dominic Bruce

OFLAG IX A 1356

Lt Bruce.
"The Devil In The Box"

• NINETEEN •
MEN OF COLDITZ

This section shows a small selection of photographs and collectables featuring the many personalities that were held in Sonderlager Colditz. Although emphasis within my collection naturally centres on the British and Commonwealth prisoners, it should not detract from the equally brave men of other nations including America, Belgium, Czechoslovakia, France, the Netherlands and Poland who formed the backbone of the camp.

One of the great personalities at Colditz was **Lt Col William Tod** and I am grateful to Barry Tod, his nephew, for giving me his photograph to include in my collection.

Both the prisoners and guards held William Tod in great esteem during his period at the castle. The Germans in particular were grateful for his handling of events as war drew to a close, which could have caused them many post-war problems. Eggers wrote that in his opinion Tod was a better officer then Prawitt. He was prejudiced against his superior officer however, whom he didn't like.

On the other hand the British officers and ORs were united in their feelings, echoed by Major Neale who wrote: "The SBO was Col Tod, a most outstanding man, I remember his first address to us when he took parade [appell]. 'When things look so bloody awful that you tend to despair the only thing to do is to retain your British sense of humour and laugh. This is the third and last Reich, its years are numbered.'"

Known as 'Tubby', **Lt Col Broomhall** made a brilliant escape from Oflag VIIB at Laufen. Dressed as a German general with prisoners dressed as Swiss representatives and German

Registration photograph of Lieutenant Colonel William Tod, Senior British Officer, Colditz 1943-1945. Also the envelope with the negative of the photograph, which he received from the Germans.

F/Lt Dominic Bruce.

Cartoons by the Colditz artist John Watton.
Top: Lt Col Tod takes the 12 noon parade.
Right: German officers take the 4pm parade.

Far right: Official photograph showing 33321 Major W.F. Anderson dated 14 December 1945, on his return to Royal Engineers barracks.

Bottom: Lt Colonel Broomhall fourth from right, Major Cleeve third from right and Major Kimble second from left. All three were destined for Colditz.

escort he managed to bluff his way out of the camp. This was during a Swiss Commission visit. He may have been too convincing for with his fluent German he berated the gate guard for being too slow in raising the barrier, in order to distract him from what was taking place. The guard however, smarting under the verbal assault, telephoned the guard commander to enquire why he had not been warned of the general's party leaving as arranged. The guard commander knew however the Commission were still on the camp with the Commandant. He rushed to the gate, then gathering a riot squad pursued the party just making for the wooded area; they were stopped and captured earning Broomhall and some of his colleagues a ticket to Colditz.

Peter Allan was one of the first two British officers to breach the walls of Colditz. Escaping on 8 May 1941 he had to admit defeat through hunger and exhaustion when being turned down

Lieutenant Peter Allan in his disguise, photographed after the attempted toilet escape. Signed post-war by Allan. This was taken from the Colditz Museum by Captain Eggers when he was destroying evidence at the end of the war.

Official identity pass issued to Squadron Leader 09334 Lockett on his return to unit on 3 June 1945.

Pair of photographs removed from the Colditz Museum by Captain Eggers. They show F/Lt Dominic Bruce and on the right a rope made from bed sheets hanging from the second window of the building on the left. This is where he escaped from after releasing himself from a nailed Red Cross packing case, which was moved to the Kommandantur building. This earned him the title of 'devil in the box'. The photograph was signed post-war.

by a concerned American consulate in Vienna to whom he had gone for help. As a neutral nation they could not take the chance of him being an agent provocateur and the police were waiting for him on his return for an appointment.

Dominic Bruce was recaptured at Danzig after escaping from Colditz. Dominic wrote: "I was awarded the AFM in June 1939 after lightning struck the aircraft. I was knocked unconscious but when regaining consciousness mended the broken transmitter and eventually bailed out with complications. Shot down in June 1941 I spent a total of eight months in solitary for escaping activities. I escaped from Spangenberg as a German pilot intending to steal a Junkers 52. I was also court-martialled for releasing POWs in solitary so they could play cards. I

escaped as a French orderly from Oflag IVB. I was then sent to Colditz in April and escaped in September of 1942. Having reached my destination of Danzig and arranged to be taken on a boat I was captured. The MC was awarded for escaping and I have been told that having an MC and AFM is rather unique."

Giles Romilly, Churchill's nephew, was the first senior hostage held for Hitler. Romilly, who had been a journalist when captured, although a civilian was so important to the Nazis they held him in Colditz. Both the Commandant and the security officer would receive an immediate court-martial if he escaped. Kept alone in a cell, he had a special squad assigned to check on him every two hours night and day. Even so he breached the walls and was nearly successful but

Above: Giles Romilly in the courtyard of Colditz.

Above right: Romilly dressed as a dame for a Colditz revue with Squadron Leader Lockett as escort. Lockett sent this photograph from Colditz to his wife. No doubt she was both amused and confused.

Right: Copy of a receipt from Dresdner bank for 10 marks sent to Colditz in November 1943. This is signed by Romilly.

Bottom: Copy of an unusual book parcel address label from France in 1944 received by Romilly.

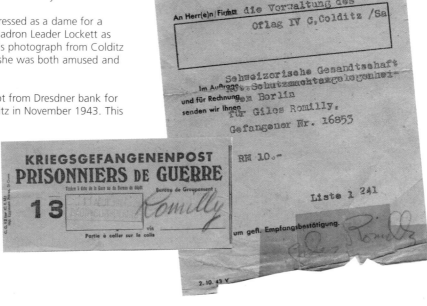

Above: The most important group photograph taken in Colditz of British officers. It is the only one that shows so many significant individuals together. This photograph, which belonged to Rupert Barry, is stamped, 'Not allowed to be posted', as the windows have obviously been obliterated to hide the bars. This picture was very popular with escapees to cut out for their travel documents. Back row, from left to right: Bill Fowler (Australian, home run), 'Pembum' How (RASC), Geoff Wardle (RN, subs), Giles Romilly (civilian, Churchill's nephew), Howard Gee (civilian, fought in Finland, captured whilst returning and suspected as Russian spy), 'Jumbo' Mazumdar (RAMC, a loyal and brave Indian officer who made a home run from another camp). Middle row, from left to right: Trooper Hughes, Pte. Scott, Monty Bissel (RA), George Skelton (RAF, repatriated), Peter Storie-Pugh (R.W. Kents), Pat Reid (RASC, home run), John Lace, Kenneth Lee, Mike Sinclair (60th, the 'Red Fox' and Great Escaper, killed 1944), Peter Allan (Cameron's, first to breach the walls). Front row, from left to right: 'Pop' Olver (DLI), Rupert Barry (Ox & Bucks), Padre Platt, Dick Howe (RTR), Geoffrey Ransome (NAAFI), Bobby Colt (Tyneside Scottish).

Left: Signed photograph of F/Lt Ivo Tonder, one of two Czech officers sent to Colditz after recapture from The Great Escape at Luft III. Ivo was a member of 312 Czech Squadron and was suspected by the Gestapo of involvement in the 'Home Army'. Held in a Gestapo prison, he was sentenced to death and sent to Colditz for further interrogations before execution. He survived the war.

was captured by the special squad. Romilly's conditions improved as the war progressed. Another Prominente, Michael Alexander shared his room. During an interview his night guard, Herr Heinrich (Oflag IVC 1942/44), a member of the special squad assigned to Romilly told me, "Romilly complained of the permanent light in his room, which was then made dim during the night. Once again he complained of my boots keeping him awake and I had to wear slippers, which I didn't appreciate in the winter."

It was in the late sixties that I received a letter from an insurance broker in France named **René Bardet**. He wrote an extraordinary story. On the collapse of the French Forces and wishing to continue the fight he 'deserted' from the Vichy Navy and fled to England and joined the Royal Navy.

Promoted to Lt Cmdr, he was given the identity of Ronald Lewis Barnet. Placed in

Dutch officers photographed by the Germans after the discovery of a second dummy the Dutch had made to assist in escapes. The Germans had christened the dummies Max and Moritz. Max was used prior to discovery, as an additional 'prisoner' for counting purposes on return from the Colditz park after an escape, and also on an appel. They were not perfect and needed to be used in poor light. The names Max and Moritz came from a German storybook for young children. Written in 1929 by Wilhelm Butch it was published in Munich and told the story of two naughty boys who always came to a bad end. The book was reprinted in 1971 and Reinhold Eggers, the Colditz security officer, who had related the story to me, gave it to my children, Kim and David that year as a Christmas present.

Colditz reunion at the Imperial War Museum. Jedrez Giertych and wife introduced to the Queen Mother, Patron of the Colditz Association.

French/British. German POW identity photograph for Lt Cmdr Ronald Lewis Barnet.

Naval officers, Colditz. Back row, from left to right: Hoggard, Barnet (Bardet), unknown. Middle row, from left to right: Harvey, Catlow, Bruce. Front row, from left to right: Beets, unknown, Moran, unknown, unknown Polish.

The night guard Heinrich (left) with another Colditz guard, Schneider (1942/3), photographed by the author in the mid-eighties.

charge of SGB7, they were on patrol in the English Channel on 19 June 1942. They had sunk a cargo vessel at Cherburg when they were joined in battle with German E-boats. Out-gunned they were eventually sunk, with the loss of two lives.

Bardet knew that if his true identity became known he would be shot for 'desertion'. He was sent to the Royal Naval POW camp named Marlag, from which he was soon to escape. Recaptured at Köln he returned to solitary confinement at Milag Nord. The Germans soon realised he was special and he was sent to Colditz. His escape activities still continued.

Bardet wrote that some of the British realised his true identity but he was never concerned that this would be revealed. He took great care to ensure none of the other nationalities got to know the truth. His friends in England were in constant touch making sure the Germans accepted his new identity.

Unfortunately he had to keep clear of the French, as he knew there were some 'inform-ants' amongst them. When liberated, René was a very ill man. He eventually returned to France.

• TWENTY •
BATTLE FOR COLDITZ

Private First Class Francis Giegnas twisted around onto his stomach on the grassy knoll and leaned on his elbows. He looked at the three PFCs with him, all members of the six-man I & R (Intelligence and Reconnaissance) section, who were 'chewing the cud'. There was Walter Burrows, who with him was a 'high point' man with longer service than the other two, Alan Murphey and Robert Miller. Giegnas himself was a tall man with a square jaw line.

"Have any of you guys got the time?"

Burrows looked at his watch replying, "It's eleven hundred hours, isn't it time you got yourself a decent watch?!"

"Yea, right," with that Giegnas turned onto his back and closed his eyes to take in the warmth of the sun and reflect on how he had got there.

It was 11am on 9 April 1945.

The four men were members of HQ Company 3rd Battalion of 273rd Infantry Regiment. Their motto was 'Steadily advance'. Being in the 273rd they had trained at Camp Shelby, Mississippi in May 1943 as part of the 69th Infantry Division, known as 'The Fighting 69th'.

After training they left New York harbour on 14 November 1944 to arrive at Southampton and Avonmouth on 26 November 1944. Travelling in convoy to Winchester they were billeted on Salisbury Plain under canvas and in Nissen huts. After the Battle of the Bulge they left England, sailing on the *Morowai* on 22 January 1945 for France; they then travelled by trucks and reached their HQ at Gourney-en-Bray on 24 January.

By 27 February 1945, 1st, 2nd and 3rd Battalions had advanced to Gescheid, Kamberg and Schnorrenberg. By mid-March the 273rd were at the River Rhine and crossed the famous Remagen Bridgehead. The Battalion crossed the River Werra and was now detached to Combat Command R, 9th Armored Division. The force was augmented with tanks and designated as Task Force Shaughnessy, after their leader.

Captain Reinhold Eggers sat at his desk and tapped a pencil against his teeth. He was worried. Knowing the war would soon reach Colditz, his concern was that he had put his trust in a young private to deliver two letters he had written on 8 and 9 April to his wife. This was strictly against orders as the Commandant Colonel Prawitt had placed a ban on anything leaving the castle that was not official on the highest instructions from SS Headquarters.

Himmler was concerned his prize hostages would come to the notice of the Allies and did not want information to be passed on. If the private was stopped or volunteered the information then Eggers would be shot immediately. But the risk was worth it just to have contact with his beloved wife. He flinched as a sharp rap on the door interrupted his thoughts.

"Enter," he barked.

A Sherman tank of 9th Armored Division is guided over Colditz bridge on 16 April 1945. Signed by Lieutenant Colonel George Ruhlen (retired as a major general), of 9th Armored Division. He visited Lt Col Shaughnessey at Colditz on 27 April 1945. Photo by US Army. (*US Army records office*).

Top left: The two Eggers letters of 8 and 9 April 1945.

Top right: Colonel Shaughnessy.

Bottom left: PFC Alan Murphey on the *Morowai* en route to France.

Opposite page: The insignia of the 69th Infantry Division. PFC Alan Murphey's shoulder patch.

The insignia is a red block '6' and a blue block '9' which interlock. No heraldic significance.

The shoulder patch was displayed on the upper left sleeve. It was worn by all members of the Division up to the time it went into combat. At that time, for security reasons, it was removed. Its display was again authorised starting 25 April 1945, on the occasion of the Division's link-up with the Soviet Army.

The 69th was organised at Camp Shelby, Mississippi on 15 May 1943. There was no 69th in World War One, although there was a New York regiment known as 'The Fighting 69th' who became famous through the James Cagney film. The 69th Infantry Division arrived in England on 26 November 1944, but did not enter combat officially until 11 February 1945, relieving the 99th Infantry in the Siegfried Line.

The Division commander was Major General Emil F. Reinhardt. Regimental commanders were Colonel Henry B. Margeson (271st), Colonel Walter D. Buie (272nd), and Colonel Charles M. Adams, Jr. (273rd).

The Division suffered 1556 battle casualties and was awarded a total of 90 Silver Stars and 1847 Bronze Stars.

Private Dire walked in and saluted. He took a letter from his uniform pocket and handed it to Eggers.

"From your wife, Captain." He added, "She sends her good wishes."

Eggers took the letter from the soldier's hand.

"Thank you Dire. How was your family?"

"As good as can be expected sir. Frau Prawitt is keeping contact with all the wives."

"Ah," Eggers murmured, "that's good. Thank you again."

Dire saluted and left the office.

It was 10 April 1945.

The four PFCs were woken early that day to the sound of Sherman tanks revving their engines and were soon ready to join the convoy on their advance deep into Eastern Germany. After three days of little resistance they came under sustained attack from SS troops with 88mm gunfire on the valley road to Altengroitzsch. The 3rd Battalion was ordered to take the town and destroy the 88s. They achieved this on 14 April with the cost of ten men killed and ten wounded.

The 69th Division was to advance and take their biggest prize – Leipzig. There was one obstacle in the way – Colditz. The 3rd Battalion was given the task with the support of tanks to take the town.

Many years ago I received a relevant extract, which would appear to have been taken from a thick US report. A note stated "After Action Report, dated 1 May 1945". The report follows.

"On 14 April at 0600 Altengroitzsch was mopped up and Groitszch was cleared. On 14 April, Battalion was ordered to move to Wildenhain. Bn reached Wildenhain without encountering resistance.

"Third Bn spent the night in Wildenhain and moved out at 1000 on the 15th. Entered Ebersbach at 1400. At 1600 Bn received orders and passed through elements of CCR to seize Colditz and liberate allied PWs.

"At 1800 co-ordinated attack was launched on Colditz. Bn attacked North with I Co on the east side of the river, K Co on the west side of the river with L Co in reserve following K Co.

I Co was unable to proceed further than the south edge of town. Colditz, east of the river, was pounded with artillery throughout the night. L Co was withdrawn from the west bank of the river and sent to reinforce I Co on the east bank. L Company, with machine platoon of M Co supporting, and I attacked abreast at dawn of 16 April. The town was cleared by 0900hrs.

"Bridge across the River Mulde was seized and found to be in usable condition.

"Garrison at Colditz surrendered and allied prisoners were liberated."

A war journal of unknown origin was discovered lying in a supply room by the acting supply sergeant of 273rd Infantry in August 1945. This together with other information came into my possession about fourteen years ago as part of a report gathered after prolonged research by Alan H Murphey.

"15 April 1945.

"At 1600 the Battalion received the following message: 'Take Colditz and release British.'

"Orders were immediately given for the attack on Colditz. From a departure point at Hohnbach, I Company was to move southeast, cross the River Mulde on a railroad bridge, which had to be taken intact, and then attack Colditz from the south. K Company was to attack that part of Colditz on the west bank of the river, and L Company was to follow K Company. Self-propelled artillery of the 9th Armored Division was in position to give support; and there was also fire on call from the tanks and Td's [small armoured vehicles] attached to the Battalion.

"By 1900 the companies were in position to launch the attack, and artillery preparations were laid down. From the start I Company had a rough time. All the resistance proved to be on the east side of the river, and the part of Colditz east of the river was by far the greater part of the town. I Company was hardly across their LD [Line of Departure] when they were met by heavy machine-gun and rifle fire. Panzerfausts were used also by the Germans in the close-in [hand to hand/bayonet] fighting that developed.

"All the assistance possible in the form of artillery fire was given to I Company, but as darkness fell it became evident that the eastern portion of Colditz could not be cleared that night. Four men, including two platoon sergeants, T/Sgt Gallagher and T/Sgt Hadaway, had been killed, and eight men, including Lt Ryan, platoon leader, had been wounded.

"Meanwhile K Company had encountered little difficulty clearing that part of Colditz on the west bank of the river. It was only when the Company approached the bridge between the two parts of the town that resistance was met. In an attempt to check the bridge, T/Sgt Miskovic was killed and another man was wounded. The German guards on the bridge were also killed.

"I and K Companies set up local defences for the night, and L Company was withdrawn to Hohnbach, where Colonel Shaughnessy gave Captain MacLane orders for an attack with I Company at daybreak."

"16 April 1945
"During the dark hours of morning, Company L crossed the railroad bridge that I Company had used, and moved abreast of I Company. Phase lines were set up by the two companies for the attack through the town.

"But an attack was not necessary that bright Monday morning. The Germans had withdrawn. A few prisoners were taken.

"A curious angle of the whole affair was the complete indifference shown to the numerous German soldiers wandering around the courtyard of the castle. This was a result of agreements reached between the German garrison and captives before their liberation. Hearing of the American approach, the garrison had decided not to put up a fight, but to surrender the castle to the prisoners and await capture. Elements of the German army that resisted the attack on Colditz had nothing to do with the Colditz garrison, and these had withdrawn to be picked up later.

"Members of 3rd Battalion, 273rd Infantry who were killed 15 April 1945, during the attack on Colditz:
Gallagher, William CT/Sgt I-Co
Hadaway, J.CT/Sgt I-Co
Miskovic, Emil M. T/Sgt K-Co
Peterson, Marvin R. PFC I-Co
Whaley, Robert G. PFC I-Co
Name unknown."

These are interesting reports as it is obvious from interviews and the fact the castle was shelled that the Americans were not aware the castle held prisoners until the tricolour and Union Jack were flown. First impressions of the advancing battalion were that it was a German garrison.

The Colditz town historian Mr Ilschner wrote to Alan Murphey in 1991: "Located in Colditz on 15 April 1945 were parts of the 101st Motorised Rifle Replacement Battalion whose garrison was in the neighbouring town of Leisnig. About 200 soldiers with tanks arrived in Colditz on 13 April 1945. During the night of 15-16 April these 200 soldiers with tanks withdrew from Colditz. Also in Colditz the so-called 'Volkssturm' existed, but no records exist."

In April 1945 the population of Colditz was 6000 inhabitants.

Lee Carson, an American Staff Correspondent of the International News Service was present with the 69th Infantry Division when Colditz was liberated. He wrote in the *San Francisco Examiner* on 18 April 1945: "The Yank force composed of tanks and infantry from the 9th Armored Division met fierce resistance by well organised bands of Hitler Youth under command of SS officers."

In fact although there were Hitler Youth present, it would appear they were not led by the SS. However, investigations suggest that the 101st Motorised Rifle Replacement Battalion, although not an SS unit, consisted of young recruits who were trained and led by SS officers. Alan Murphey found that this was common practice towards the end of the war. This could be why SS units were thought to be in Colditz town.

Elwell Meadows, one of the American GIs, wrote in 1994:

"Our advance liberated many foreign workers who had been sent to Germany to work. There was no organised effort to assist these people. We gave them what help in the way of food and medical assistance we could. At one point, a number of Poles joined our company and followed along behind us. They were headed east which was the way we were going. I suppose they felt safer being near us and I cannot think of a more effective military escort than a company of American infantry, armed to the teeth. They had obtained a large American flag, which they carried at the head of their column. The only member of our company who could talk to them in their native tongue was the 1st Platoon sergeant, Emil Miskovic, a Polish-American from Chicago. We jokingly called this ragtag army that followed behind us, proudly displaying Old Glory, 'Sgt Mick's other platoon'.

"By the time we got to Colditz, alas, Sgt Mick's other platoon had deserted to a man.

"We entered Colditz along the west bank of the river late in the afternoon. My platoon, the 2nd Platoon, was short on leadership because our platoon sergeant had been seriously wounded and the assistant platoon sergeant had been killed in a firefight a couple of days before. The 1st Platoon was in the lead, ahead of us.

"We got word that the 1st Platoon had run into trouble at the bridge that spanned the river and we began to be harassed by sniper fire. We ducked into a nearby factory building. I do not know what product was manufactured in this factory but the machinery appeared to be new and of modern design. The workers had assem-bled at long tables on the second floor of the building in what had been their dining area. I went upstairs to see if I could get a better idea from an upstairs window of where the sniper fire was coming from. (We thought it was from a tower on the other side of the river.) When I reached the top of the stairs, loud cheering and handclapping startled me. Then I realised that I was the first American the workers had seen and that they were all cheering me. I gave them a 'thumbs-up' sign and motioned for them to be silent and to stay where they were until the danger had passed.

"Darkness had fallen by the time we had got to the bridge where we learned that Sgt Mick had been killed. Our medics took him to a building across from the foot of the bridge, but Sgt Mick had died instantly from a bullet wound to the head. A young German lay dead at the foot of the bridge.

"Our platoon bedded down for the night in a building a few doors up the street from the bridge and posted a guard at the bridge during the night. The Germans had erected a makeshift barricade from metal debris across the approach to the bridge. Wind blowing through the metal debris made a creaking, groaning sound. As I stood my watch, by the first light of the day I could make out the forbidding outline of the structure on the other side of the bridge – my first glimpse of Colditz Castle. The bridge had been partially destroyed but was still passable to foot traffic. I did not know where the weapons platoon or the rest of the company was at this time. I assumed that they had crossed the bridge earlier in the night.

"In the morning, at perhaps eight or nine o'clock, a horse-drawn hearse, an ancient conveyance that looked like a stage prop from a Wild West movie, came and removed the young German's body. A woman whom I assumed to have been the boy's mother accompanied the hearse. Her grief and bereavement were genuine, but I could not help thinking that her son would not have died if he had been at home where he belonged.

"As the morning wore on, throngs of people appeared in the streets near the bridge — refugees fleeing the advancing Russian troops

Allied Hostages Hidden In Nazi Redoubt Area

By LEE CARSON
Staff Correspondent Int'l News Service

WITH UNITED STATES FIRST ARMY IN GERMANY, April 17.—Twenty-one prominent British and American prisoners have been taken to Adolf Hitler's headquarters in the so-called national redoubt as hostages, units of the American First Army discovered today.

An American task force sent across the Mulde River to seize a Nazi camp for "special enemies of Germany", and free the hostages, arrived forty-eight hours too late.

While the other prisoners were sleeping, the twenty-one hostages were taken from their cells, chained together and loaded into a truck for their trip to Hitler's last-ditch refuge.

DRIVE BY TANKS—

The Yank force composed of tanks and infantry from the Ninth Armored Division drove to the camp despite fierce resistance by well organized bands of Hitler Youth under command of SS officers.

Every town on the road had to be fought through, but in less than twenty-four hours the tanks, with doughboys riding topside, blasted their way through the prison barriers and broke down the gates of a medieval castle which had served as a prison camp in two wars.

The twenty-one hostages were gone. They were Allied officers who earned their place in this sink-hole by trying to escape or by refusing to give information, by their excellent battle records —or by reason of prominence.

Five American officers, including a colonel who had been sentenced to die, were rescued along with 350 British, a thousand French and a handful of Poles whose number had been gradually whittled down by SS pistols or starvation.

Lt. Col. William Herbert Schaefer, of Carmel, Ill., had been sentenced to death for protesting against Nazi posting of an abusive notice announcing that any prisoner attempting to escape would be shot.

'RESERVED' CELLS—

The reason given was that "Americans have violated all the rules of warfare and there is no longer any reason why Germans should obey the rules or show any mercy to any member of the Allied forces."

Colonel Schaefer was captured July 14, 1943, during the battle for Bascari in Sicily. He has been dragged through most of Germany's worst prisons and concentration camps, ending up in this one, which was reserved for "worst offenders and most valuable hostages."

Senior officer among the Americans was Col. Florimond Duke, who parachuted into Hungary just after Budapest had launched separate peace negotiations.

With Duke were Capt. Alfred M. Suarez and Capt. Guy T. Nunn of Los Angeles, Calif.

The three parachutists were kept by the Gestapo for six months, during which time all the abuses and tortures of which the Nazis are past masters were used to break them down.

"They kept us handcuffed with our hands behind our backs," Colonel Duke said.

"We got no mail in or out, and no cigarets. We were kept in solitary confinement cells and never permitted to speak to one another. When we were moved we were chained together like a Georgia road gang."

who were not far away at this time. This was in sharp contrast to the eerie emptiness of the night before.

"Then we began to see prisoners who had been liberated from the castle. I talked to some of them. They said they were members of the British Red Devil Airborne Division and that they had jumped at Arnhem in Holland. I hope that the prisoners of Colditz will not forget the life of Sgt Mick and the sacrifice he made for their liberation at the stone bridge before Colditz Castle on 15 April 1945."

Glenn Oliver wrote of how it felt to be in I Company in the battle for Colditz:

"I Company, 273 Infantry, moved into position to take Colditz on 15 April 1945. It was late afternoon on a beautiful day. The tank commander who told us that there would be no problem taking Colditz met us. As we left the trucks and moved forward on foot, we crossed a bridge. A fellow soldier from Ohio asked about a German lighter, which he wanted. I told him to wait until after the battle. We marched up the road and could see dust flying off the ground. The Germans were firing on our men. At that time we were facing a large embankment. Orders came to attack and we climbed up the embankment and went down into a field. We were ordered to open fire. I fired the first shot and my rifle jammed. The Germans opened up with terrific fire. My friend from Ohio was hit and later died. I moved back to remove the cartridge from the magazine with a machine-gun ramrod.

"Firing was so severe and close that lying in a prone position, my sergeant's canteen was shot. Another friend from Greencastle, Pa. was shot but didn't die. Machine gunners moved up and quite a few were wounded. We could not move forward because of severe firepower from the Germans.

"Orders came to move back and the artillery was called in. We could not take

Newspaper report by Lee Carson.

Left: The River Mulde near the point where the Americans crossed to the east side and met strong resistance.

Below: Woods in background where American artillery was concealed.

The Adolf Hitler bridge with the damage found by the Americans. Photograph taken at first light on the morning of 16 April 1945. (*Meadows*)

Colditz until the next morning, 16 April. Many men were wounded and died.

"I did get a new rifle."

PFC Robert Hoffman, Light Machine Gun Section, K Company, wrote:

"K Company entered Colditz along a railway track. I Company was on the other side of the river. We took heavy machine-gun fire and could hardly move. I did manage to look up at the guy lying ahead of me. He was gesturing to me to look back to my left side. In my haste to seek protection in the culvert, I had laid my 30 cal. light machine gun upright along the embankment so as to protect the barrel from dirt – the gun stood out like a flag and could be seen by the Germans. I slid the gun down to me and crawled forward. The firing soon stopped. We decided to make a run for it and on a signal clambered up the embankment, through a field of high grass to the protection of the roadway. When we reached the road we were giggling like idiots. We couldn't stop laughing. The machine-gun fire was coming from a tower and the trajectory of the fire was level with the grassy field we were running through. The sound of the bullets ripping through the tall grass which seemed to be all around us and none of us being hit, set us up to laughing. It's hard to rationalise; it wasn't funny, yet to us at that moment it was.

"Later, when we moved into the town towards the bridge, we lost Sergeant Miskovic. I believe he was from New York City, a little older than most of us and well liked by his men. A young boy, possibly fourteen or fifteen-years-old, dressed in a German soldier's uniform stepped out of his doorway and shot the sergeant in the head. The rest of his platoon fired at the boy and he lay in the roadway in front of his home.

"This was at the base of the road that crossed the bridge over the Mulde. Half of the bridge was blown away, but it could still be used by driving on the sidewalk around the hole in the middle of the bridge. I had set up my machine gun to fire across the bridge. As I Company was still in action on that side of the river, our side was basically secure. Germans tried to cross the bridge to our side and some surrendered when

confronted, others ran back. That went on for a short time until the other side was secured. That's the side of the river with the castle and where the POWs were liberated.

"A Frenchman approached me. He was wearing a Red Cross armband. I believe he had been interned in the castle. He was a very gentle person and asked if the mother of the boy, who could be heard crying and peering from the window, could secure his body and prepare him for burial. It was very sad.

"As the day progressed and the sun rose higher, it got very warm and I was waiting to be relieved. During this time, a number of Germans surrendered, others were flushed out of cellars. A very official and important looking person was brought in on two occasions. He wore a green uniform with which we were not familiar. He looked like a general. I speak a little German, not much, but enough to learn that this guy was a mailman. We released him. When he was brought in the second time, he was quite annoyed and made no bones about it. He mumbled something like 'stupid Americans'.

"We took over a house of a man who worked with zeppelins. He was not there but his two daughters were. In the basement were many kinds of food preserved in jars of brine. They tasted good so we had a feast, with wine, of course. The guest of honour was our own Colonel Shaughnessy. Sergeant John Hahn was the instigator and chief cook."

Staff Sergeant Roy Verdugo wrote:

"On 15 April Tech Sgt Hadaway, whom we called 'Pappy', along with Tech Sgt Gallagher and I, were going to celebrate Pappy's birthday as soon as we took Colditz. Sgt Gallagher's 1st Platoon was the left pincer, Pappy's platoon, the 3rd Platoon (ours), the middle, was to draw fire, in the open meadow. 2nd Platoon was the right pincer. We started on the attack, my first scout was hit and was very lucky. I had given him the signal to move about fifteen paces and as he started to get up, a bullet went into his shoulder blade, missed his spine and went into the other blade. My rifle was sticking, resulting in improper firing, so I grabbed my scout's rifle and left him mine. I told him to lay still, not to move, assuring him that aid men would be along soon. Then Whaley got hit somewhere in the belly and died the following morning. I was unable to see Whaley but the aid men told me that the bullet did not go clear through him.

"We were about 40 or 50 feet from the front slope to the meadow when Pappy, to my right, got hit. He was laying crossways from where the firing was coming. I could see dust in front of and behind him. I knew he was a goner, as he was not moving. There were so many bullets coming at us that the trees were crackling like they were on fire. The bullets were so close to hitting me that I could feel the whizzing next to my ears. Next thing I knew I felt something cold running down my fanny. A bullet had hit the top of my canteen. It's a good thing I had an aluminium top and not plastic. Then, my other scout got hit and he wanted water, which I did not have, it had all run down my fanny. I had two bandoleers of ammo and a gun belt. I turned my helmet crosswise allowing me to aim and fire; otherwise my neck would push the helmet over my eyes. I was afraid to take it off due to the chances of being hit by shrapnel; I used all my ammo. Captain had sent us a bazooka to fire but I had only fired a bazooka once and couldn't remember how to wire it. We withdrew to reorganise and sent for more ammunition. During this time they brought in a lieutenant with an eyeball hanging out of its socket (shrapnel had got it).

"We reorganised and my platoon formed a defence for a counter-attack. It was dark when my Captain moved us to a building close by and gave me orders to stay outside until further notice. A patrol had gone over the bridge and a young German was lying there wounded. We stayed outside the building, cold and nervous, and my men begging to go inside. Finally, I decided to go check it out and I found it was safe enough. So, I placed three guards outside and let the rest of the men go on in. Anyway the Captain came back a few hours later and wanted to know who gave the orders to occupy the building, I told him I did but he refused to listen to the reason."

James Telenko wrote:

"I was a twenty-year-old Squad leader of 3rd Squad, 2nd Platoon, K Co and I was checking on 3rd Squad members, who along with a 30 cal. machine gun from our heavy weapons platoon were guarding the west end of the bridge. It was 15 April 1945. It was just before dusk when someone started walking towards us from the east end of the bridge. The person appeared to be wearing a bandanna over their head and a short cape, so we thought it might be a woman. The sound of his hobnailed boots on the surface of the bridge negated any hope they had concerning a disguise.

"The person was allowed to advance within earshot when they were ordered to halt. We removed the cape and bandanna and found we had a Hitler Youth captive. I questioned him about the size of the German garrison on the other side of the bridge without any success. I left him and rejoined my troops, as I had to organise the bridge guard roster for the night.

The 'Helmattum' tower. Source of withering machine-gun fire that took its toll on I and K Companies.

The next morning, 16 April, I saw the body of a youth about sixteen-years-old laying face down on the bridge. He was taken away by 3rd Battalion ambulance."

Bob Hoffman recollects the Hitler Youth he had dealings with at Colditz:

"A Hitler Youth had been shot after he shot Sgt Miskovic in the head. One of our machine guns was set up at that spot and of course we had to stay there. The youth had been taken into a house and later the mother came to me with his cap containing bullets [which must have been taken from his dead body]. She looked at me with contempt so I merely took the cap, dropped the bullets into the river and returned the cap to her and told her to go inside. I was only nineteen-years-old and this was not easy.

"After being relieved my squad went up the hill in the direction of the grassy field. We were standing in a group when someone noticed a group coming towards us out of a wooded area. They looked like a Boy Scout Troop, with flags and pennants. We recognised them as Hitler Youth boys. They were very frightened when we approached them. They did not carry any weapons. We determined that they were local boys and told them to go home."

Robert Muckel of I Co 273rd Infantry Regiment wrote in 1994 of his experiences during the liberation of Colditz:

"On 15 April 1945 I was a nineteen-year-old PFC in 1st Squad of 3rd Platoon. We approached Colditz in trucks and came to a stop at the top of a hill. We had a pretty good view of the area directly in front of us. At the bottom of the hill was a small river. On the opposite side a grass-lined bank slowly inclined upward to a hill covered with trees. On the other side of this hill was the town of Colditz which our division was about to attack. On our right a small railway bridge spanned the river, this appeared our only way to get across the river. We walked down the hill, crossed the bridge then turned left walking along the riverbank. After a short time, we made a right turn, and headed up the hill. After reaching the wooden area at the crest of the hill we spread out in a long line side by side and lay belly down on the grass under the trees.

"On our front the woods sloped gently downwards and gradually the trees thinned out and there was a large open grassy area. The Germans were out there someplace and well hidden, we did not know where they were, but they knew our exact position, and were probably watching our every move.

"Off in the distance on our right front was a large gray building, which looked like it may be some kind of factory. We were still lying on the ground when one of our officers made a motion with his hands, to fix bayonets. I thought to myself, uh oh, here we go. After putting our bayonets on our rifles, we looked back at the officer, he raised his arm in the air, and slowly threw it backwards, then quickly thrust it forward, and shouted all right, lets go! We got up off the ground, and began our charge down the slope. No one talked or made a sound, it was real quiet. How far down the slope before the Germans opened up on us with their machine guns, I do not know, but open up they did. The bullets were coming at us like swarms of bees. Some of their guns must have been firing high, because as we ran, I saw small twigs from the tree limbs overhead that had been shot off and were falling down around us. Suddenly one of non-coms hollered out, fall back, fall back, we all then turned around, and started running back up the slope as fast as we could go. Speaking for myself, when we began that charge, it seemed like everything changed from reality to a dream. My mind was detached from my body. As I ran down and back up that slope I had no feelings or sensations of my feet ever touching the ground.

"Reaching the top of the hill, we ran back down the other side a little ways so as to be hidden from the Germans' view and gunfire. Here we stopped and everyone began looking at their clothing and equipment for bullet holes. Our platoon sergeant, Pappy Hadaway, had us assemble around him, and told us in case he got hit in any action to come that he was now naming someone else to take over his job as head of the 3rd Platoon.

"Pappy was only twenty-six-years-old but he had the respect of the whole platoon. Always a smile on his face, he always seemed in complete control and never had a harsh word for anyone. As he talked one of the men suddenly appeared saying that German soldiers were encircling us. We had the river behind us and no more of our troops could get over to reinforce us. Pappy Hadaway told two of us to go back down the hill towards the river and find a good spot. Watch out for the Krauts in case they came behind us. We lay there a long time, it got dark and then we heard shouts and shooting from the top of the rise where our company was located. The noise went on for a long time then there was quiet. At last came the light of morning and we couldn't keep the suspense any longer and went up to make contact with our company. Close to the top of the hill we found some members of our company, from their faces we knew they had been in a hell of a fight. I asked where Pappy was and was told he was not with us anymore. One member said they were cut off and surrounded in a field, where most of the action took place. Our wounded lay there and the Germans walked amongst them kicking them, any who screamed were finished off. One of the men played dead and managed to crawl out after they had left. Because the men were in a state of shock I stopped trying to get any more information and walked over the other side of the hill towards the town of Colditz."

An article that was written on the liberation of Colditz suggested a GI by the name of Peterson had been reported Missing Not Traced. Alan Murphey received a letter in 1992 from a William Armstrong, which read:

"I may be the person who was listed as missing in action. I was advancing under fire with I Company, 2nd Platoon, 3rd Squadron when as we got into Colditz a bullet entered my upper right arm. My battle jacket also was penetrated by at least six other bullets. One went into the centre of my turned up collar and it never touched me.

"As I was lying on the ground a medic gave me morphine and said he would be back. After some five minutes I crawled across the street and into a basement. When the small arms fire let up, I made my way down the hill and started up another steep hill to our original position. On the way I came upon a non-com helping a badly wounded sergeant, (I think his name was Reinhart). All the wounded were directed to the other side of the ridge to await evacuation. We were taken by ambulance to a farmhouse and laid on stretchers for the remainder of the night. The next morning we were fed and our wounds attended too. We were then taken to a grass airfield and C47s took us either to Paris or Liège. I went to Paris. We landed at Orly Airfield and I was taken from there by streetcar to the First General Hospital located in Vitre sur Seine. I spent several months in hospital and upon release made my way back to I Company which was located at a German airfield. My parents were informed by telegram that I was missing believed dead."

Record of HQ Company 3rd Battalion, 273rd Infantry Regiment:

"15 April. Moved from Wildenhain at 1045 and arrived at Leupahn at 1740. Distance about 27 miles. Have 17 men from Colditz guarded in a barn believed to be prisoners of German Gestapo. Released in the morning. [These men were left for dead at the concentration camp Colditz by their SS guards. As no one was able to communicate with them they remained under guard until their identities were verified. They were then hospitalised before assisted on their way.]

"16 April. Moved to Colditz at 0915 and arrived at 1320. Distance 5 miles. Captured 24 Germans in woods around Colditz. One German shot while trying to get away."

• TWENTY-ONE •
LIBERATION OF COLDITZ CASTLE

During my research I endeavoured to trace the four American GIs the British officers had reported as liberating them on the morning of 16 April 1945. I knew that Pat Reid had made contact with Alan Murphey, one of the four that was serving at that time in Germany, who related his story. However, this had been understandably fairly sketchy, as Colditz, although shown as one of the battle honours of the 69th, paled in comparison to some of the other major battles they were involved in, including Leipzig and of course the historic meeting with the Russians at Torgau.

I was fortunate enough to be able to trace Alan, but was very lucky to find that as a result of that original contact it fired Alan to dig deeper into those days at Colditz.

Alan was a natural and very methodical investigator and the story of the American involvement at Colditz is revealed as a result of his research. The fact that he passed on all this information to me first hand, for the purpose of this book, shows how unselfish he was in his research.

His achievement in making contact with Bob Miller, another of the 'four', gave him the greatest of 'kicks' and he was bubbling over in his letter when he related that they had met for the first time since the war. After trying so hard to locate them, Alan had to concede that the other two would never be traced.

I had related my 'finds' to the secretary of the Colditz Association, Kenneth Lockwood, and he then told me a forgotten story, which was quite amazing: "There was another chap who came in you know that morning. I remember him quite clearly, he opened the door at the entrance, walked in, then when he saw us all turned tail and beat a hasty retreat. It must have been about an hour before the other four arrived."

This must be one of the most bizarre stories regarding the liberation of the castle and I was determined to find out the facts. I related the story in an article that I wrote on Colditz to the 69th Infantry Division magazine. As a result the following reply appeared:

"Ex PFC Robert L. Muckel I Co.273rd Inf. Regt. On page 47 of the sixty-ninth bulletin I read a story, by Michael Booker. Near the end of the story, they mention a lone GI who entered the castle via the wicker gate at the main entrance. Well, I think I may have been that fellow.

"I entered Colditz through a small square that was filled with German soldiers, all standing there with both hands over their heads. American soldiers had raised rifles pointing at them, guarding them. I kept walking and came to a hill on the left-hand side. Near the top was a large building with what looked like big barn doors, I thought to myself this may be another German army warehouse. Maybe it's filled with

Drawing by John Watton made of PFC Giegnas as he entered the castle to the cheers of the prisoners.

PFC Robert L. Muckel.

wine and brandy like the last one I opened up.

"I turned the latch holding it closed and slowly opened the door. It was real dark inside. I could hardly see but as my eyes slowly adjusted to the darkness I could see that the whole place was filled with soldiers, most of them sitting on the ground, some were standing up. My first thought was boy I am in trouble now. The place is filled with German soldiers. But on closer inspection, I did not see any rifles or arms anywhere. On top of that their uniforms looked like those of the British Army. These men must be British prisoners of war held by the Germans. And if that is the case then the German guards must be close by. Otherwise why are they still locked up?

"As the men inside looked at me none of them spoke to me and I in turn said nothing to any of them, but I do remember the smiles on a lot of their faces when they saw me. I did not enter the building more than a foot and I did not speak as I did not want to make any noise and alert any guards who might not be aware of the fact that our troops had taken the other side of the town. And if the guards saw an armed

American soldier standing there by the open door, I would have a hard time trying to explain this to them while they were shooting at me.

"Not knowing the true situation I thought it best to get the heck out of there and fast. I thought I'll leave it to the prisoners, they now know the American Army is here and they can take over from here. I left the door hanging open, turned around and headed back to my company."

As part of I Company, Muckel had entered from the eastern end of Colditz. The German soldiers he saw as prisoners of the Americans, from my research of a plan of Colditz dated 1936, would have been in the 'Sophienplatz'. Muckel in his narrative mentions, "our troops had taken the other side of town". Leaving the square he would have walked along 'Sophienstrasse' into the top part of 'Untermarkt', and from there into the 'Markt' and on to the castle.

Here are the recollections of Alan H. Murphey:

"I was a member of the battalion Intelligence and Reconnaissance [I&R] section. Other members of the section present with me at Leupahn were Private First Class Walter V. Burrows, Francis A. Giegnas Jr., and Robert B. Miller.

"A soldier sent by the first sergeant awakened us about 5am on 16 April 1945. 'The first sergeant wants to see someone from the I&R section.'

"Burrows said he would go. When he returned, he told us that the first sergeant had received word from Colonel Shaughnessy at the Forward CP that he wanted us to set up an observation post. Our instructions were to proceed east on the road out of Leupahn until we reached the River Mulde. There, we were to turn left (north) and follow the river until we reached a bridge. Once there, to occupy a building overlooking the bridge with a good view of the town, and await the arrival of the battalion comm section who would run a wire and provide a field phone. But when the comm section would arrive was not specified.

"I do not remember receiving any information on the whereabouts of our own companies or of German units, other than that they occupied Colditz. No mention was made that there was a prisoner-of-war camp in Colditz.

"Burrows, Giegnas, Miller and I set out from Leupahn about 6am. We carried nothing but our M-1 rifles. We wore steel helmets and had on M-43 field jackets with the standard M-1 ammunition belt around our waists. It took us about an hour and a half to reach the Mulde. We heard no gunfire and saw no American units. Soon after turning north towards Colditz, we met a civilian who turned out to be a Frenchman. He approached us coming from the direction of Colditz. He identified himself as a prisoner-of-war, but he was dressed in civilian clothes.

"I talked to him in French, that surprised him. I believe he was an ex-POW who had been released from camp after volunteering to work in Germany. It was from the Frenchman that we learned of Colditz Castle. He told us that there were Allied officers being held there, 'des prisonniers trés importants' he told me. After leaving the Frenchman we heard a couple of rifle shots. They were coming from the east bank of the river, near the Colditz bridge, which we could see ahead of us. We could clearly see the outline of what was obviously Colditz Castle, which the Frenchman had told us about.

"When we reached the bridge, we saw our first Americans, a half dozen infantrymen crouched behind a parapet that bordered the bridge's west bank. A sergeant gestured us to take cover. We ducked into the closest building facing the bridge. While Miller and Giegnas ran upstairs to see if the building was suitable as an observation post, Burrows and I crouched in the doorway.

"A minute or two later we saw a German soldier running across the bridge from the east bank waving a piece of white cloth. When he reached the west bank, a couple of infantrymen grabbed him, pulling him below the parapet. From the doorway, we could see the sergeant talking to the German. A half minute later the sergeant yelled, 'Any of you speak German?'

"'I do,' answered Burrows and made a short dash to the stone parapet. I could see Burrows talking to both the German and the sergeant. Then Burrows beckoned me to join him. I ran the few feet it took to reach the parapet. 'The German says his unit has pulled out of Colditz and the town wants to surrender. But the sergeant doesn't want to cross the bridge.'

"'Why not?'

"'There are still snipers over there,' said the sergeant. 'I'm not going to risk my men.'

"Burrows looked at me, 'You want to try it?'

"'I'm game, let's check with the others.'

"I shouted to Giegnas who by then was crouched in the building's doorway. 'Come here and bring Miller.'

"The four of us held a miniature war conference behind the wall. But within a few minutes we decided to cross. It was one of those quick decisions that you often have to make in combat.

"We raced up onto the bridge roadway. We had to jump over a dead German youth sprawled on his back to the left of a gaping hole in the roadway (an earlier unsuccessful attempt by the Germans to blow up the bridge, we learned later).

"The street starting at the other end of the bridge veered to the left. When we reached it we saw white sheets hanging from almost every window. We spread out in a single file. I believe Miller was at the front of the file. I took up the rearguard position. We walked about 300 feet when I looked over my shoulder. My heart almost stopped. About 150 feet behind me, I saw three German soldiers double-time across an intersection we had previously passed. The lead soldier carried two ammo canisters, one in each hand. He was haunched over and running fast. Directly behind him were two more soldiers carrying a machine gun mounted on a tripod. The soldier in front ran with his hand behind his back holding the gun barrel. The soldier behind held two legs of the tripod.

"We continued our walk until we reached a large square [the market square]. We stopped and stared across the open expanse. The square was completely deserted.

"Suddenly the stillness was broken by the crash of falling shells. We ducked into the doorway of a house. We realised that our own 105mm howitzers were shooting at us. It was obvious that no one knew that we were in the town and that the shelling was a softening-up barrage, in preparation for an eventual attack.

"I think at that moment we all realised that we were supposed to be back on the west bank of the Mulde reporting observable enemy activity, assuming of course, the comm section had shown up. For a moment, I could visualise the section being court-martialled.

"But we had gone too far to turn back. We stood in the doorway for no more than a couple of minutes, although it seemed an eternity. It was immediately apparent we needed to escape the shelling. I do not remember who suggested the castle, but a quick decision was made to make a run for it.

"We dashed to the closest street exit to our left. After a short dash up the narrow street, the castle came into view. I was struck by the imposing size towering above us. We reached what appeared to be a sentry gate, but it was unguarded. We crossed a moat bridge and

The narrow street that Murphey and his companions dashed up to avoid the mortar fire. This ended with steep steps, which led to the castle approach. The small Colditz cinema, apparently visited at least once by the prisoners of war, is at the end on the left.

entered a covered passageway under a clock tower. It was dark and musty smelling. Ahead of us we saw a wooden door. I believe I opened it. There, a few feet from the door, standing in a large courtyard, were two groups of men. To the left, about five or six British officers, to the right, about a dozen German officers.

"A second later it became obvious that the two groups were awaiting our arrival. A young British officer stepped forward and grasped my hand.

"'Welcome to Colditz. We've been waiting a long time.'

"The other officers stepped forward and introduced themselves. In the excitement of the moment, I did not recall their names or their ranks, except for an American colonel by the name of Duke.

"I remember an officer stating that a number of prominent prisoners had been evacuated a couple of days earlier, including Polish General Bor of the Warsaw uprising and Winston Churchill's nephew, adding there were over a thousand Allied officers left in the castle.

"When we asked where the prisoners were, they told us they were restricted temporarily to their quarters. Our conversation quickly moved to the immediate situation. We were told the German officers wished to surrender. Miller, noticing they were wearing pistols, suggested they be disarmed. Burrows, in German, asked them to turn over their sidearm.

"Reluctantly, each officer removed his pistol from its holster.

"'Aren't they're any more Germans?' asked Miller.

"'They're confined to their barracks,' replied one of the British officers.

"Again, Miller was anxious to gather up all arms. Burrows asked for the senior German officer to order the surrender of all arms. The German officer turned and shouted across the courtyard. We saw a German standing in the doorway of a building bordered by a terrace [the Kommandantur] pass the order into the building.

"What happened next was a shock to the four of us. We stared in disbelief. Across the courtyard streamed a mass of German soldiers carrying rifles, literally hundreds of them. One of the

British officers suggested we direct them into a room under the clock tower.

"Miller and I stood inside the room, obviously a guard's room, as the Germans poured through the small doorway, directing them to stack their weapons on the floor.

"I remember one old German in particular. He was about sixty. After throwing down his rifle, he stopped in front of me. He pointed to a gas mask in his hand and raised his shoulders questioningly. I gestured for him to throw it in the pile. He flung the mask on the floor and gave me a broad smile. While Miller and I were in the guardroom, Burrows, Giegnas and the British officers directed the German guards exiting from the guardroom to seat themselves on the grass lawn in front of the Kommandantur.

"The weapon stacking probably took about ten minutes to accomplish. Burrows then suggested that he escort the German officers back to the west bank of the Mulde and get word back to HQ that we were in control of the castle. We agreed and Burrows left with the German officers in tow.

"One of the British officers announced that he would take us to meet the senior allied staff. I remember him specifically saying the senior French general was waiting to meet us. Miller said he would remain to guard the prisoners and weapons. Two or three British officers joined him. I believe the building they led us to was to the left as you faced the courtyard, although I am not positive on this. We climbed a staircase to the second floor. There we entered a long room with windows facing the outer courtyard. I remember there was a long table and behind it a fireplace with an ornate mantel. There was also a large portrait of Hitler hanging from the wall. A number of officers stood in the room.

"Giegnas and I were introduced and we shook hands (again, I remember no names). I do not remember the exact protocol, but I believe the French general was the first officer to whom we were introduced. I greeted him in French and he was delighted. He asked me where I had learned to speak with such a good accent. I replied, 'à l'école à Geneva en mille neuf-cent trente-cinq, mon général'. I believe he asked us our branch of service and unit designation.

The four reached the top of the steps that led to the approach road and entrance to the castle.

"Giegnas and I answered a number of questions posed by the staff. We were in the room about ten minutes, when Giegnas turned to me and said, 'Ask the general if we can have the picture of Hitler.'

"The general if I remember correctly answered Giegnas directly in English. 'Of course. Take it.'

"Giegnas then turned to our British escorts and asked if they would take us to the prisoners. We left the building and walked through an arched passageway that led to a narrow entrance gate to our right. Passing through the gateway we emerged into an inner courtyard. As we stepped into view a roar of cheers greeted us from the countless windows overlooking the yard. I could see faces at every window. Also, small groups of men in the courtyard. Giegnas raised the picture of Hitler high above his head with both hands. He turned in a slow arc so that all could see. Then, he crashed the picture across his raised knee. There was pandemonium. The shouts and cheers echoed in the narrow confines of the courtyard.

"It was soon after this dramatic scene that we were introduced to Lieutenant-Colonel Schaefer, an American officer. It is my recollection we met under the arched passageway on our way back to the outer courtyard, but I could be mistaken. I also believe we were told that he had just been released from his solitary confinement cell, where he had been awaiting execution. Colonel Schaefer did not look well. His face was pale and his hands shook. I could see tears on his cheeks.

"Soon after Giegnas and I returned to the outer courtyard where Miller and a number of

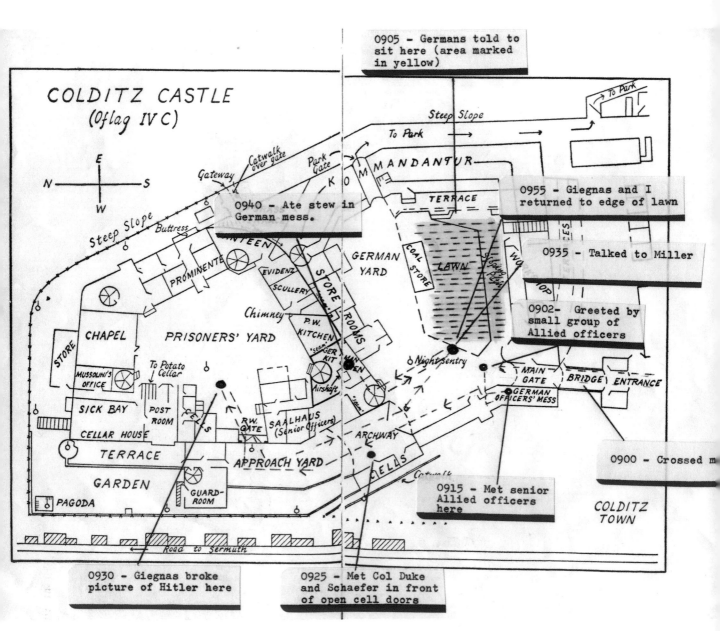

Sketch plan of the castle completed by Murphey of times and events within the castle at liberation.

British officers still guarded the German prisoners. Miller said some of the Germans wanted to eat. We decided to allow them to leave and eat in small, unescorted groups. We realised that if an individual soldier really wanted to escape he could find a way to do so. There just were too many Germans. Guarding them was merely a symbolic gesture at this point.

"'I'm starved too,' said Giegnas. 'Where's the kitchen?'

"A British officer pointed to a doorway across the yard.

"'Let's go,' said Giegnas. I followed him but Miller said he wasn't hungry.

"I believe the entrance was close to the arched passageway leading to the inner courtyard. I am sure, however, we climbed a steep, circular staircase to reach the German mess. We entered a room with arched ceilings. A young German stood behind a short serving line with a ladle in his hand. In front of him was a large aluminium pot. When he saw us, he almost dropped the ladle. We gestured we wanted to eat. He took a bowl, ladled in the scoop of what appeared to be stew and started to pass it to me. An older man, apparently the mess sergeant, rushed up and grabbed the bowl. He yelled something at the young German. I thought for a moment that he had told him not to serve me. Instead, he added more stew until it almost ran over the top of the bowl.

"Giegnas and I walked to a table close to an archway and sat down, leaning our rifles against the table. There were about four or five German soldiers in the room eating. They stared at us and whispered to each other as we ate. The stew consisted mainly of potatoes, but did contain pieces of what appeared to be beef. As we ate, Giegnas commented that we were probably the first Americans to eat with the Wehrmacht.

"When we returned to the outer courtyard, I would estimate it was about ten o'clock. We stood for a moment at the edge of the grass lawn talking to a British officer, Miller suddenly joined us with a small penknife in his hand. 'One of the Germans was trying to cut his wrist, but it's only a superficial cut.'

"'Which one?' asked the British officer.

"Miller walked back a few feet along the side of the seated prisoners. He pointed to a German in the centre of the row holding a handkerchief against his wrist.

"'That one,' said Miller.

"'He's the Colditz executioner,' remarked the British officer, 'just keep an eye on him.'

"It was very soon after that other American troops entered the courtyard. I do not know what time it was. I do know that we had been at Colditz for about an hour when they arrived."

Following are the recollections of Robert B. Miller:

"We had come down a plateau towards Colditz from our side of the Mulde with orders to set up an observation post. Seeing a few houses on our side of the bridge, we thought one of these houses would be an ideal place for our observation post and afford a little protection for us. On reaching the bridge I looked across, seeing part of the left hand side of the bridge was destroyed and a dead German soldier was lying on the bridge. We then saw a 'one-armed' man standing on the other side, I believe he had his good arm in the air in surrender. He came across the bridge to where PFC Walter Burrows was and he talked in German a few minutes. Then Burrows told us that the town wanted to surrender and he would guide us.

"After a debate we decided we would go and take a chance. Also at this time there was a lot of artillery fire. We crossed the bridge and walked up the road on the left. We then walked up a steep road to the castle for shelter. When entering the castle there was a bridge of thirty to forty feet, there were two rooms on either side, which we assumed were guardrooms. When going across the bridge and under the arch there was a large building. This was later used as the command post for our Headquarters Company. The castle surrendered to the four of us. As the town was still being shelled Burrows said he would return to tell them to stop the shelling and inform them that all had surrendered in the castle. We informed the Germans we wanted all arms collected and brought to the room on the left by the archway. I stayed in the room as the weapons were brought in. I had collected many pistols, securing them with two or three pistol belts around my waist. In addition to the two bandoleers of M-1 ammunition crossing my chest, I had two grenades within the chest pockets of my uniform. After all the weapons were brought in, filling up the room completely, I went back to the courtyard and joined PFC Giegnas and PFC Murphey. Giegnas had taken a picture of Hitler and standing in the middle of the courtyard had proceeded to put his foot through it. Wild cheering through the barred windows showed approval of this gesture.

Shortly, PFC Burrows arrived with officers and newspapermen plus more of our company's men. The castle began to fill up quickly after that. As the prisoners were being released, we began chatting with one another. They were quite anxious to take us to the top of the building. Under the sloping roof they showed us the glider they had built. I assumed it was built of wood and it was covered with a blue and white cloth. It was quite amazing! They had fixed the roof so it could be propped open and had

The liberation photograph. Taken seated outside the castle it shows PFC Burrows standing, PFC Murphey standing and looking to the right, (while smoking a pipe and wearing a liberated German army belt), PFC Giegnas facing forward smoking a pipe, and PFC Miller on the wall holding a book. (*R. Miller*)

intended to send the manned glider across the Mulde. They also showed me a secret room under the floorboards with a map on the right wall showing the advance of the allied army. They had a radio on the table and had been receiving information to keep their map up to date. It was quite a remarkable task and effort these men had attempted.

"The photograph of the four of us was taken on the wall outside. On our right was the guard house building we came through to get to the courtyard. Either PFC Juan Pizarro or PFC Clinton B Dirmore who made up the other two members of our six man Intelligence and Reconnaissance squad took it. Captain Hotchkiss as Battalion intelligence officer was in charge assisted by Sergeant Nystrom.

"One thing I remember quite well, I was quite impressed by one gentleman. His name was Flight Lieutenant Chalupka and he was from Czechoslovakia and had been a prisoner in Colditz. Murphey and myself had been asked to escort him into town. He was to meet with another gentleman who was to become the burgomaster when the allies took charge of the town. This gentleman was a Clark Gable type, the black hair, good-looking etc. It felt like we were making a movie. The home of the burgomaster was very beautiful, I really hated to enter his home as dirty as I was or sit on his furniture and drink a glass of wine.

"We stayed in Colditz a few days and then moved on."

The four liberators were awarded the Bronze Star for their heroic actions. Alan Murphey wrote:

"My Bronze Star citation states that our section was manning an OP 'which was under heavy fire'. Manning is rather a definitive word to describe our brief occupancy of a building at the bridge. 'Under fire' is pure fantasy.

"The citation continues to say that we 'learned that a large enemy force was moving into a fortress-like castle'. If anything, the opposite was true. We entered the town because the German soldier had said his unit had departed. It appears the writer of the citation, whoever it was, wanted to provide us with a motive, prefer-

ably courageous, to cross the bridge. 'A large enemy force moving into a fortress-like castle' met that requirement. That we subjected ourselves to 'friendly as well as enemy fire' is only half-true. The only fire we underwent was from our own howitzers. The citation also implies that all of us returned with the information the garrison wished to surrender. In fact, this would only apply to Burrows."

Alan Murphey in one of his last letters wrote:

"I can say without reservation that the liberation of the castle was my finest hour during the Second World War and I shall always remember the warm and heart-wrenching welcome I received from the prisoners."

Citations for G.O No 64. Hq 69th Inf Div. 18 June 1945

Private First Class Alan H. Murphey, 42064823, Infantry, United States Army, for heroic achievement in connection with military operations against the enemy, on 16 April 1945, in Germany. Entered military service from New York.

Private First Class Walter V. Burrows, 33425492, Infantry, United States Army, for heroic achievement in connection with military operations against the enemy, on 16 April 1945, in Germany. Entered military service from Pennsylvania.

Private First Class Francis A. Giegnas, Jnr. 12100663, Infantry, United States Army, for heroic achievement in connection with military operations against the enemy, on 16 April 1945, in Germany. Entered military service from New Jersey.

Private First Class Robert B. Miller, 33837074, Infantry, United States Army, for heroic achievement in connection with military operations against the enemy, on 16 April 1945, in Germany. Entered military service from Pennsylvania.

There was of course a great deal of interest in Colditz Castle from those 'in the know' and

HEADQUARTERS 69TH INFANTRY DIVISION
APO 417   U S ARMY

18 June 1945.

SUBJECT: Award of Bronze Star Medal.

TO   : Private First Class Alan H Murphey, 42064823,
           Infantry, APO 417, U. S. Army.

CITATION

Private First Class Alan H Murphey, 42064823,
Infantry, United States Army, for heroic achievement
in connection with military operations against the
enemy, on 16 April 1945, near **** Germany. While
manning an observation post which was under heavy fire
during the attack on a well-defended town, Private
First Class Murphey and his three companions learned
that a large enemy force was moving into a fortress-like
castle. Fearlessly crossing a bridge into enemy territory, the four men subjected themselves to friendly as
well as enemy fire as they made their way to the castle,
occupied by more than three hundred of the enemy and
more than a thousand imprisoned Allies. At the risk
of their lives, they conversed with the enemy commander
and returned with the information that the garrison
wished to surrender. His courage and initiative reflect
the highest credit upon Private First Class Murphey and
the armed forces of the United States.

By command of Major General REINHARDT:

H. PENGELLY,
Lt. Col., A.G.D.,
Adjutant General.

Copy of Bronze Star citation issued to Alan Murphey.

influential journalists had been attached to Shaughnessy's staff in anticipation of the liberation of Colditz and the castle. Unfortunately communication seemed to have broken down in the heat of battle and the ground troops were unaware of the importance of the prize.

Therefore when four GIs were credited with taking the surrender of the castle then Lt Col Shaughnessy had some explaining to do. One GI sent to the castle with him wrote that a female journalist dressed in a boiler suit gave a very embarrassed colonel a hard time as they approached the entrance.

Colditz Castle was officially surrendered by the Commandant Colonel Prawitt to Lt Colonel Shaughnessy. When a British officer asked where the four Americans were who had liberated the castle, he was told they were engaged on other important duties. In fact they were having their photograph taken on a wall of the castle!

If the officer who wrote the Bronze Star recommendation had told the facts as they happened, the surrender of over a hundred armed German soldiers in a fortress to four men, what would the bravery award had been then I wonder.

The surrender did in fact hit the headlines of the British and American Press. The *New York Times* and *San Francisco Examiner* printed the news on 18 April 1945 written by Staff Correspondent International News Service Lee Carson.

The *Times* of London also printed it the same day from *Times* reporter Michael Burn, direct from Colditz.

Louis Sarube wrote: "I was a Staff Sergeant Wire Chief for Regimental HQ Wire Section 271st Regt. When I arrived at Colditz I knew of the castle which we could see on the hill, but had not been told it had been a prisoner of war camp. We were there for about ten days from 2 May 1945. Our code name was 'Trespass'. I had twenty-six men in my section. There were four jeeps with trailers and our job was to get wire communications to our Regiment, behind right and left.

"The house I chose as our HQ was right behind the railway station. The reason for this was because it was empty. Although I hated the Nazi soldiers I did have compassion for the ordinary citizens. My orders, which I passed on to my men, were no fraternising with the Germans. Do not eat German food or accept their drinks. Do not wander off alone. Do not mention casualties to Germans. Check all papers of anyone over 12yrs and see they are the proper ones. Anything you find locked must be opened, doors, drawers and other locked articles."

On the subject of the Germans in the town, Ewell Meadows wrote:

"The night we entered Colditz, Jim Telenko, a member of my platoon, was given the assignment of finding a place for us to bed down for the night. Jim performed this task with dispatch, if not enthusiasm, by evicting a lady from her house near the bridge. Ordered to vacate her premises on very short notice, the lady, like

The gravestones of the four Americans killed at Colditz. (*Mario Bosch*)

Queen Victoria, was not amused. As she was leaving, the dear lady insulted us: she said we were behaving like Germans."

PFC James Eyster, L Company, 273rd Infantry, wrote of the death of FDR: "We had just had two days of bloody fighting against the SS and on arriving at Colditz I was met by one of the French prisoners streaming from the castle. He embraced me with tears and said how sorry he was for the death of our President. I told him he must be mistaken, as we had not heard anything."

Maj Gen Ruhlen wrote on the capture of Colditz: "Our Combat Command Reserve (CCR) captured Colditz on 16 April. CCR was subdivided into at least two task forces named Deevers and Shaughnessy after their respective commanders. Each had companies from the 2nd Tank Battalion attached to them. I visited the place two or three days later. There is a photo of one of our tanks crossing the bridge and entering Colditz."

I have the following letter regarding the official surrender of Colditz amongst my correspondence. Unfortunately I cannot read the signature.

"Our 3rd Battalion, 273rd Infantry, 69th Division, under the command of Colonel Leo W.H. Shaughnessy, captured Colditz in April 1945. I was, at that time, the Battalion S-2 Intelligence officer. However, at the battalion level a more accurate description would be a patrol leader. Also, at that level of involvement during the battle for Colditz, my role was more that of an ordinary infantry lieutenant.

"I was fortunate to be with Colonel Shaughnessy in the German general's dining room for the fortress during his surrender. [This of course refers to Colonel Prawitt.] He gave his sabre and pistol to Colonel Shaughnessy as a token of surrender. His wife and daughter [son] were there. Later, he escorted us around, showing the rooms where the officer prisoners were billeted. Also, he showed the 'museum', if that is a correct term, of the various means of failed escape attempts.

"Several American officers were under sentence of death because of previous escape attempts. They were extremely happy to see us. I was told that only officers were imprisoned there and were there because of escape attempts from other POW camps.

"The 273rd Infantry Regiment was not involved in administration to any extent. We left Colditz soon after its capture and continued to take our assigned part of Leipzig. Subsequently, the 273rd Regiment met the Russians at Torgau. I want to add that in visiting the various rooms of officer POWs the English officers were outstanding in their attention to discipline and dress though their uniforms were tattered, or in rags. Many had been prisoners for five or more years."

The following letter I received from Michael Kutzmonich of Wapwallopen, PA. He writes of the days after the liberation of Colditz and has a fascinating group of photographs of the Russians when they entered Colditz.

"I was in a heavy weapons company. I was assistant gunner on the 81mm mortar. Being in a motor company we would travel north or south to help the rifle companies. Each platoon had four squads and each squad had a jeep and trailer to carry the ammunition.

"Sometimes we were in the 1st Army and sometimes in the 3rd. Most of our Division was going to Leipzig and as we had just finished we went south.

"I don't recall how long we were in Colditz but as soon as the 69th met the Russians at Torgau, the Russians kept coming to their own occupation zone, they were all right behind us and they would put up a little shanty town at all roads. One thing I remember about Colditz. On 8 May 1945, VE day, I went to the church to thank God that I made it through the war. My one buddy from the state of Washington followed me in. He did not pray, he went up the altar, looking for wine, he found a bottle and as he stepped from the altar he turned around and held the bottle up and said, 'I hope the good Lord forgives me, but we can use it more then he can.' When we came out of the church we had a good drink to celebrate VE day."

James Kidd wrote:

"I was the leader of 1st Platoon, F Company, and 271st Infantry Regiment. Around the end of April our unit was relocated to Colditz, and my platoon was given the duty of guarding the bridge in the centre of town that crosses the River Mulde. The bridge had a large hole blasted in it near the middle, but vehicles could cross the stream if care was taken. We were instructed to be alert for the arrival of Russian units on the east side of the Mulde. They arrived a couple of days after we got there.

"We were in Colditz when the news of the German surrender came. One morning just at daybreak a Russian lieutenant arrived at the bridge and said he had some artillery on the American side of the Mulde a few miles away and he needed permission to return them to the Russian side. He wanted to take the pieces across the bridge at Colditz. I told him to bring them along and cross there as I was sure the bridge would take the weights. No, no, he said. He must see the colonel to get permission. I took him to the battalion commander at his headquarters about half-mile away; the colonel, of course, told him the same thing as I did. A few hours later the artillery pieces came rolling down an unpaved road. Steam tractors, diesel tractors and trucks pulled them. They crossed the bridge without a problem.

"By the way, my soldiers and the Russians had a great time showing off their weapons to each other. They went a way along the riverbank and fired each other's weapons. Our men were especially intrigued by the submachine gun with the round magazine."

In conclusion to the American action in Colditz, Alan Murphey came up with this interesting information on the burial sites of

Staff Sergeant Sarube (seated on right) on Colditz station yard in April 1945. *(Sarube)*

some that were killed at Colditz.

Four out of the six men killed at Colditz are buried in the Netherlands cemetery at Margraten, 6 miles east of Maastrict. All were members of I Company. These are:

T/Sgt William C. Gallagher. ASN 36100300, from Michigan, died 15 April 45. Buried in Plot A, Row 12, Grave 25.

T/Sgt J.C. Hadaway. ASN 38300774, from Texas, died 15 April 45. Buried in Plot L, Row 12, Grave 21.

PFC Marvin R. Peterson. ASN 42132525, from New York, died 15 April 45. Buried in Plot I, Row 2, Grave 3.

PFC Robert G. Whaley. ASN 36832692, from Wisconsin. Died 16 April 45. Buried in Plot K, Row 7, Grave 22. PFC Whaley died on 16 April of wounds he received on 15 April during the attack on Colditz.

The British view

Lieutenant Grismond Davies-Scourfield kept a diary of events in Colditz. Below are two extracts:

"15 April 1945. Inspected the countryside at 7am – a beautiful morning, but no sign of the war. At 8.45 Thunderbolts appeared low overhead machine-gunning. A wonderful sight. The village emptied rapidly and there was no sign of the Volkssturm. At 8.50 six Thunderbolts dived right across the village and fired on the station. Tracer and spitting MGs were clearly visible. Micky Burn tried to get a car to go through to Königstein last night to make contact with the Prominente. Very plucky. But the Brigadier rightly forbade it. At 11.30 went up into the attic. All quiet but tanks visible at the southern end of the woods 2 miles away. Great speculation as to which nationality. Three German tanks can be seen in the village. We could see their gun flashes. At 2.20 the SBO ordered us down on to the ground floor. Bits of shells have come through the attic roofs. There is quite a lot of noise. At 2.38 the Germans blew up the bridge, but so ineffectively that the traffic could still pass. One Frenchman in the attic has been hit in the ankle by a piece of shell. At 3.10 shells began to burst quite close. We have hoisted the Union Jack, Polish and French flags. American infantry were seen just before dark crossing the river south of us and soon vicious MG fire could be heard on the high ground behind us. We slept in our usual rooms to the sound of shells passing overhead.

"Monday 16 April 1945.

"There was no battle. In the early light American troops could be seen cleaning up the town. There was the occasional burst of small arms fire. The only opposition came from one house, and heavy mortars quickly silenced that. David Walker was sent out with Eggers to contact the Americans and announce that the Commandant wished to surrender the castle. They had an adventurous trip but made contact. Americans came up, liberated us and received a tremendous ovation. We were free at last."

Photo showing Mike Kutzmonich (left), a Russian soldier, and John McGlatz on the east side of Colditz bridge with castle and church up the hill. April 1945. (*Kutzmonich*)

Colditz bridge early in May 1945. American and Russian soldiers and two East European women. The soldier third from right is a South African who joined the American Army in England when they arrived. (*Kidd*)

The German view

Reinhold Eggers also kept a diary of events in Colditz.

"15 April 1945. Sunday. The spring sun rose in the blue sky. No bells rang in the village to call you to church. About 10am five American tanks came out of Colditz forest and crept up to the village. They fired and some houses burst into flame. Suddenly a sharp crack in the castle of a shell exploding, time to leave the windows. Then Douglas Bader's room was hit, fortunately no one was in there. Then we replied with three cannons from somewhere in the Tiergarten. The Americans were not troubled by this and replied with heavier shells that fell in Colditz and in the castle. The only casualty was Feldwebel Bar, who was crossing the outer courtyard when a shell fell, killing him. The Commandant's rooms were struck. The Americans were not crossing the Hitler bridge, which should have been blown. They crossed the river by a railway bridge where the machine-gun nests were situated. Fighting became furious during the night.

"Monday 16 April 1945. Captain Pupcke came to the Commandant with a suggestion by the SBO that the Union Jack and tricolour be raised. This was agreed to. The firing stopped. We learnt that a lieutenant saw the flags and immediately ordered the firing stopped. About 10am an American sergeant [PFC Burrows] accompanied by one or two privates entered the German yard by the stone bridge. We were assembled there. I went to him and informed him that this was Oflag IVC, that there were no prisoners injured and handed him a complete list of them all. I introduced him to the Commandant. The sergeant decided that all the German officers should remain where they were and that I should accompany him to his captain bringing with me the list. He pointed to my revolver, which I had forgotten to lay aside, I did so now and followed him out. The streets were empty. Here and there an American guarded an important place. On crossing the bridge I saw the poor attempt that had been made to blow it up, only half of it was damaged. On the far side lay three men of the 'Volkssturm'. One of them was about seventeen-years-old, lying behind a primitive shelter of harrows and barbed wire. We went to the last house in Colditz town where I saw the captain in charge of the unit. He was satisfied that no prisoners were injured and told me to return and order everyone to stay there until a staff officer arrived to take the formal surrender. I went back with the sergeant. I told Col Prawitt and Tod what had happened and together we showed them and General [Brigadier] Davies with other staff officers the German side of the camp. On reaching the officers' mess we saw that a damaged picture of Hitler was still hanging, together with a small print of Frederick the Great. General Davies, although he was lord of the castle so to speak, asked if he could have it as a souvenir. Col Tod wisely controlled his men and only allowed a few to leave the old part of the castle. We waited and waited. I went to the cellar where I slept the night. I had my breakfast there and on going to the yard found it empty, all the German officers had disappeared. They had been taken to the commander of the fighting unit, Colonel Shaughnessy. I at once hurried to leave the castle, as I was the only English-speaking officer should the Germans be questioned. Col Tod, who asked me where I was going, stopped me. I'd forgotten that now I was a prisoner. On explaining the situation he supplied me with an English guide, Lt David Walker. Walker asked me to walk behind him. As we passed the market square an American told me to put my hands up. In the Baderstrasse Walker told me to put my hands down. We crossed the bridge and came to the American headquarters.

"I saw some German staff officers standing in a line facing a slight ridge and an American soldier walking up and down behind them, I was terrified. I was roughly pushed over to Colonel Prawitt, who asked me, 'What does this mean?' I was searched and then Lt Walker returned. I asked, 'Are we safe now?' He replied that he had been ordered to find some accommodation. He returned shortly and we were taken to the upper part of a house. A sentry was placed in front of the door and from time to time civilians, whom I didn't know, were brought in to look at us. Later a soldier called out for the Commandant and security officer. We were taken by jeep to regimental headquarters at Ballendorf. Later in a large room we were introduced to two officers who gave us a meal of white bread, butter, milk, cocoa, ham, cheese and cigarettes. They then questioned us about the Prominente. We told all we knew and they then returned us to our staff at division where we were again questioned separately. No meal here. We were later sent to an old barracks surrounded by barbed wire with soldiers guarding it. A new life as a prisoner.

"Frau Prawitt who had been present with her husband and child at the surrender was then taken to one side by an American officer and given a document. This was an order to treat the wives of the German officers at Colditz Castle with respect and that Frau Prawitt as the Commandant's wife was their representative.

"This order was respected and Mrs Prawitt told me that after questioning, the wives who lived in the western zone of Germany were allowed to return there. Those in the eastern zone had to remain. Although Mrs Prawitt did not live in Colditz she had to remain there after the Russians arrived. They did not know where her husband was and hoped that he would return to her, they wanted him badly. He never returned but eventually they were reunited."

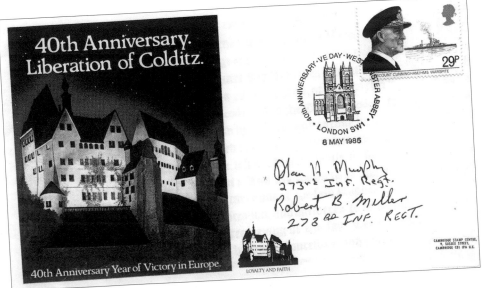

A commemorative cover celebrating the fortieth anniversary of the liberation of Colditz Castle. Signed by Murphey and Miller.

AN ESCAPE ATTEMPT IS THWARTED

The camp order displayed has been written in French. It seems to have been put together by a German without a strong command of the language. Below is a summary of the order, translated by D. Baxter. It would have been displayed on the prisoners' noticeboard.

"A group for construction will be formed under orders to repair damage to an escape tunnel discovered on 16 June 1944. The group will consist of one senior officer and three junior officers. The four officers will be together in a separate barrack. The canteen will be closed temporarily during that period. Costs for the repairs will be paid by the six prisoners responsible for the tunnel: Major Lorraine, Captain Baxter, Flight Lieutenant Bruce, Lt Barnet, Lt Cocksedge, Bosun Chrisp.

Colditz, 19 June 1940.

Signed Vogt, Sonderführer [censor department]."

Eggers wrote in his diary:

"29 May 1944. Lt Hamilton-Bailey was surprised in the locksmith's workshop by the locksmith and arrested. The prisoner had entered from a hole in the old Polish Other Ranks' quarters to the roof above the prisoners' canteen. A hole had been made through to the old Dutch quarters and a ladder used to gain access to the adjacent stairs. From there he gained access from the Kommandantur to the store."

The diary continues: "1 June 1944. Major Anderson and two other officers were surprised digging a tunnel below the dentist's chair."

I suspect that Major Anderson, as a Royal Engineer officer, was the senior officer mentioned in the camp order, and the other three officers were the two he was captured with, together with Lt Hamilton-Bailey who was involved in the canteen route.

The diary continues:

"16 June 1944. On my return to Colditz from Sagan I was in time to see a long-awaited attempt. We had recently placed an extra guard between the approach yard and the German yard, where a door was situated. This door was kept locked. During the afternoon this sentry heard some noises from beneath his feet. Nearby was the last gully-hole of the canal, coming from the prisoners' approach yard. From here pipes of about 10 inches in width went westwards under the building down into the town. The sentry sounded the alarm and we raced to the spot. On looking into the gully-hole we saw a man standing in the stinking mud and trying to make a tunnel along the pipes. At once we opened the other lids in the direction of the yard. Out of there came Major Lorraine, Captain [Bosun] Chrisp and Lt [F/Lt] Bruce. It took some time to get them out during which time Paymaster Heinze, as usual very interested in escape attempts, looked down into one of the gully-holes and spat saying 'swine'. Later the prisoners complained about this and the Commandant ordered Heinze to apologise. When we had the three 'escapees' out we put them face inwards to the Saalhouse wall so they couldn't signal anyone, as we did not know where the entrance to the tunnel was. We sent a man, armed with a rope and electric lamp, into the last gully-hole before the yard. He discovered there was a shaft going up into the wall of the canteen. The wall being 150cm thick, the end of the shaft could only be in barrack room 155, the long room, now unoccupied. I went there at once with three guards and was just in time to see three officers closing the shaft entrance after securing their escape tools. I arrested them and now knew the entrance. This escape threw some light on other escapes under construction in the shower room and the delousing shed near the Saalhouse. The aim had been to enter the canal, which had been stopped."

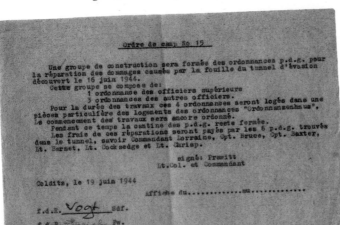

Ordre de camp No. 15

Une groupe de construction sera formée des ordonnances p.d.g. pour la réparation des dommages causés par la fouille du tunnel d'évasion découvert le 16 juin 1944.
Cette groupe se compose de:
1 ordonnance des officiers supérieurs
3 ordonnances des autres officiers.
Pour la durée des travaux ces 4 ordonnances seront logés dans une pièces particulière des logements des ordonnances "Ordonnanzenhaus". Le commencement des travaux sera encore ordonné.
Pendant ce temps la cantine des p.d.g. reste fermée.
Les frais de ces réparations seront payés par les 6 p.d.g. trouvés dans le tunnel, savoir Commandant Lorraine, Cpt. Bruce, Cpt. Baxter, Lt. Barnet, Lt. Cocksedge et Lt. Chrisp.

signé: Prawitt
Lt.Col. et Commandant

Colditz, le 19 juin 1944

Affiché du.............au.............

f.d.R. Vogt Sdf.

f.d.R. _____ Pw.

EGGERS' DIARIES

In 1960 Reinhold Eggers transferred the twenty-six copybooks he wrote on his war years, including those pertaining to his duty at Colditz, onto foolscap paper. The transfer was made in English, a difficult task considering it was not his native tongue.

The revised diaries were then used for his book *Colditz, The German Story*. Eggers obtained the services of an excellent German speaker and Colditz veteran Howard Gee, who used the diaries to edit the book.

During the late sixties Eggers asked me if I could arrange for the English version of the diaries to be checked and re-written. I used the services of George Peskett; proud of the fact he was the first English bus inspector in Berlin and master of the German language.

He did an excellent job whilst I was relegated to the laborious job of typing it on to A4 paper.

Reinhold Eggers then paid the first of two visits as a guest in my home. We called on his publisher together, armed with the revised diaries. I was able to advise them on the current interest in Colditz and how my collection had been consulted in relation to a TV series to be filmed. This resulted in an agreement being reached with Eggers on a sequel to his first book.

Colditz Recaptured was published in 1973. This used original stories provided by Colditz veterans. I was asked to make some contacts with contributors and the only person to understandably refuse was 'Solly' Goldman, much to the regret of Eggers who tried everything in an effort to change his mind, without success.

It was intended to use the revised diaries to edit the book for dates and locations. Eggers was at that time in conflict with Howard Gee, his previous editor and asked me to take on the job. I declined as a Colditz veteran was needed and John Watton accepted the task.

The diaries were next used by Pat Reid for the 1985 publication of *Colditz The Full Story*. As for the original copybooks of the diaries, they now reside with the remainder of the Eggers collection in the German National Archives.

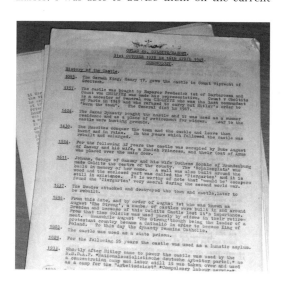

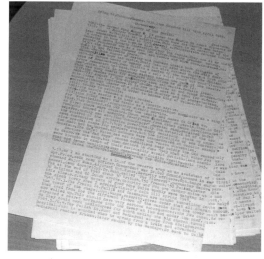

Left: The 1960 version of the diaries.

Far left: The revised version of the diaries.

ART AT COLDITZ

There were a number of artists of various nationalities held at Colditz Castle during its period as a POW camp. Major Anderson, Lord Haig and John Watton were prominent among the British contingent.

John Watton stands out for his work that appeared on a number of occasions in the *Illustrated London News* during the war. He was also the main contributing artist for *Detour* and produced post-war drawings for Pat Reid's books *The Colditz Story* and *Latter Days at Colditz*.

1. John Watton in 1977 (on right), at his home in the Lake District, during a visit by the author.

2. 'The Train Jumpers', the original watercolour that was copied for the book cover of *Detour*.

3. 'Rupert Barry kindly assists elderly guard.'

4. 'Lens Making'. Telescope making was a popular pastime in Colditz.

5. 'Entertaining a Chinese Officer'. This was adapted for use in *Latter Days at Colditz*.

6. Thumb sketch of John Watton drawing a subject. This was sent to his wife.

7. Lord Haig. 'Solitary Confinement'. A figure form drawing in black and white chalk by Earl Haig whilst a POW.

HISTORY OF THE COLLECTION

The collection has been shown in various exhibitions over the years, and for the BBC TV series on Colditz. These have also been, at times, opportunities for the Colditz veterans to get together for a reunion.

1. Original photograph of the collection of escape equipment displayed in the security officer's museum at Colditz Castle during WW2. The items shown include Pat Ferguson's distiller pipes and a turning lathe together with fake German belts, holsters and rifles.

2. A BBC TV film set for the *Colditz* series. The collection was used for authenticity.

3. A small corner of the storeroom that houses the author's collection.

4. Imperial War Museum showing the collection, exhibited in association with the *Radio Times*, 1974.

5. Lady Neave and Major General 'Tubby' Broomhall view the author's collection on display at the Imperial War Museum exhibition in 1985.

6. A reunion of Colditz veterans at the Imperial War Museum in 1985. Amongst those in the photo are, front row from left: Pat Reid, Gris Davies-Scourfield, Hugh Bruce, Joseph Tucki, Lady Neave, William Broomhall, Jack Best, Mike Moran, Micky Winn, Jim Rogers, Peter Allan.

EPILOGUE

Collecting Colditz and its Secrets has been the account of a collection. It has not tried to give a chronological history of the castle during World War Two which has been attempted by others. The collection has been my main source of reference, together with articles I have written or contributed towards and the knowledge I have gained over the period of my collection. The reader may recognise some items that I have agreed to be printed or displayed over the years, but generally the material is previously unpublished.

This then ends the story of *Collecting Colditz*. With the passing of the sixtieth anniversary of the castle's liberation, will the memory of what happened there in World War Two fade away?

The answer is a resounding 'no'. In many ways the story has not ended yet, as the power of the written word keeps the memory and discussion alive, and still more memories may come to light in time.

Sadly, it was announced in November 2004 that the Colditz Association was disbanding, however many will strive to ensure its memory does not fade. The Imperial War Museum's archive material and regular exhibitions on prisoner-of-war camps, including Colditz, will help to keep the heritage safe.

The history is also perpetuated in the castle itself. The Saxony government, which has responsibility for Colditz and other castles, takes its task seriously. An official has been put in charge of castles and under his control Colditz Castle is being renovated. It will once more display its rich history with pride whilst offering a haven for youth as a hostel.

There is also an original display from the Colditz Wehrmacht museum of World War Two. This will remain a permanent fixture and is already a major tourist attraction.

Finally, historians and collectors will continue to gather facts and mementos and be willing to share their knowledge with current and future generations. I hope in my own small way this book has been a fitting tribute to the Spirit of Colditz.

INDEX